Veil Politics in Liberal Demo⌣

In this exciting and challenging account of the development and sustain-
ability of the liberal democratic state, Ajume H. Wingo offers a completely
new perspective from that provided by political theorists. Such theorists
will typically argue for the basic values of liberal democracies by rationally
justifying them. However, there is a significant gap between what people
are rationally justified in believing and what they are actually motivated
to do. Neglect of what actually motivates us to political action carries a
great risk by leaving the motivation of citizens open to manipulation by
opportunists.

This book argues that it is non-rational factors – rhetoric, symbols,
traditions – that more often than not provide the real source of motivation. Drawing from both historical and philosophical sources, Wingo
demonstrates that these "veils," as he calls them, can play an essential
role in a thriving, stable liberal democratic state. This theory of veil politics furnishes a conceptual framework within which we can reassess the
role of aesthetics in politics, the nature and function of political myths in
liberal democracies, and the value of civic education.

Ajume H. Wingo is Assistant Professor of Philosophy and Senior Fellow
at the McCormack Institute's Center for Democracy and Development,
University of Massachusetts, Boston.

Cambridge Studies in Philosophy and Public Policy

General editor: Douglas MacLean, *University of Maryland, Baltimore County*

Veil Politics in Liberal Democratic States

AJUME H. WINGO

University of Massachusetts, Boston

With Preface by
JEREMY WALDRON

CAMBRIDGE
UNIVERSITY PRESS

PUBLISHED BY THE PRESS SYNDICATE OF THE UNIVERSITY OF CAMBRIDGE
The Pitt Building, Trumpington Street, Cambridge, United Kingdom

CAMBRIDGE UNIVERSITY PRESS
The Edinburgh Building, Cambridge CB2 2RU, UK
40 West 20th Street, New York, NY 10011-4211, USA
477 Williamstown Road, Port Melbourne, VIC 3207, Australia
Ruiz de Alarcón 13, 28014 Madrid, Spain
Dock House, The Waterfront, Cape Town 8001, South Africa

http://www.cambridge.org

First published 2003

Printed in the United States of America

Typeface Palatino 10/13 pt.   *System* LATEX 2$_\varepsilon$ [TB]

A catalog record for this book is available from the British Library.

Library of Congress Cataloging in Publication data available

ISBN 0 521 81438 3 hardback
ISBN 0 521 89128 0 paperback

To my matrilineal ancestor, Ngonnso,
my late father, Wirngo,
and to Anna, Wirndzenyuy, and Leopoldine
– to my source and destination

In order that we should love our country, our country ought to be lovely.
                                                                  – Edmund Burke

Contents

Contents

Preface

Jeremy Waldron

Maurice and Hilda Friedman Professor of Law,
and Director of the Center for Law and Philosophy,
Columbia University

Liberal political philosophy sometimes seems beset by a curiously naive literal-mindedness. We write as though the tasks of politics were reducible to the choice of principles, and as though principles formulated in the theorist's study could constitute the basic structure of a well-ordered society. We know, of course, that the articulation of principles for a liberal order is a tricky business; they have to be sensitive to all sorts of things, such as the tensions between liberty and equality, equality and opportunity, rights and efficiency, and stability and justice. And so we spend years – collectively we spend decades or generations – debating them, elaborating them, refining them. All this is done in the hope that *if only we could get the principles right*, we would have a basis for a decent, just, and prosperous social order, which could be enshrined in our laws and constitution.

Occasionally, in the wee small hours of the morning, it occurs to some of us that principles, formulated and refined by theorists, are not necessarily the key to a well-ordered society; laws and constitutions are often eclectic and half-coherent accumulations of wisdom rather than embodiments of well-worked-out principles; and anyway, laws and constitutions are not all that there is to social order. There is also the real world – the world of human nature in its more sordid or less calculable aspects, the world of chance and fortune, of crime, fanaticism, and war, of tears of pride and rage, the real world of faith, patriotism, and other creeds we would like to be able to dismiss as non-rational. Sometimes, it seems, these make a mockery of our devotion to principle-mongering. One response to these misgivings is to attempt a further refinement of our principles – attempting to make them more sensitive to various issues and vicissitudes of the real world. We might incorporate incentives into our theories or make greater provision for exceptions or sanctions or

xi

whatever. But a response of that kind seldom allays the nocturnal misgiving. What torments some of us is the possibility that there might be something wrong with our entire orientation to politics. For example, there might be something awry with the idea that governance shares with theory an orientation *towards propositions*. Let me explain what I mean. A principle is a normative proposition that says that things ought to be thus-and-so. A law inspired by a principle is supposed to be an imperative proposition: Let things be thus-and-so (and let this-or-that person be responsible for making them thus-and-so). And the law (and the principle it embodies) is supposed to work when things actually *are* thus-and-so, that is, when the society in question is actually governed, through its laws, by the principles we have formulated in the way that the principles say it ought to be governed. Maybe – and this is the thought that, as I said, comes to us in the small hours of the morning – there is more (and less) to the good ordering of society than this. Think of it this way: A society is not just a set of states of affairs, corresponding (or failing to correspond) to the content of a given set of normative propositions. It is a congeries of relations, dispositions, and emotions that are implicated with one another and with shared arrays of fear, hope, and history, in ways that defy any tidy propositional scheme. Now perhaps it is the error of communitarians and nationalists to pretend that this congeries represents an homogenous body of experience rather than something rich, ragged, and variegated. But liberal political philosophers are always in danger of making the opposite mistake – of thinking that it can be ignored altogether, or simply dragooned into the service of efficiency or justice.

These thoughts are not original. Since Edmund Burke complained about "all the decent drapery of life" being "rudely torn off" by those who would reduce the science of government to a priori speculation, there has been no shortage of critics to challenge liberal theory on this ground. They line up around the block. But there has always been a shortage of thinkers willing to do the hard work of giving an *affirmative* account of what is supposed to be lacking in the liberal picture, thinkers who are not content merely to carp, but who set out to show what a richer and more adequate philosophy of politics would look like. Ajume Wingo is one of the very few who are willing and able to do this, and for that reason I believe this book marks the emergence of a refreshing new voice in political theory.

As you read on into *Veil Politics*, you will find a deep, subtle, and sometimes disconcerting account of the role of myth, symbolism, monument, and ritual in modern politics. Much of it is about the United States: Dr. Wingo begins at the Lincoln Monument and proceeds down the Mall to end with some reflection on the racially rather sanitized depiction of American history in the rotunda of the U.S. Capitol. In between, you will read about classroom history, war memorials, the inscriptions on our currency, the Confederate flag, the Great American Seal, and the Gettysburg Address. These are sites and emblems of a politics – and of a kind of legitimacy – that goes much deeper than proposition or principle. "To make us love our country," wrote Burke, "our country ought to be lovely." Well, these are places where the love is elicited or withheld, and where loveliness or its opposite are put on display for all to see. It is places like these we must recur to if we want to develop an aesthetics of governance.

But I don't want to give the impression that *Veil Politics* is just about America, or that the part that is about America is an uncritical celebration. Quite the contrary – this book is also an account of the evasion, shame, dispute, and false consciousness embedded in this country's iconography. What Wingo insists, however, is that these too are not just matters of the truth or falsity of propositions, or the satisfaction or violation of principles. They are not just about what lies behind the veil; they are features of the veil itself.

And *Veil Politics* is not just a study of America. The fact that it is above all a work of theory – a fine work of political theory – is an irony, I guess, in light of the way I began these comments. But Wingo has succeeded not just in his critique of contemporary theory; he has succeeded in his ambition to theorize the very matters whose absence from our conventional theorizing is the premise of his work. The veil politics of the United States may be the starting point, but what is important about this book is the reflection that they stimulate and the way that Dr. Wingo is able to fold that reflection back into the traditions and experience of existing theory, to complement it and enrich it. He is helped in this by a remarkable openness and generosity of spirit. I mentioned already that Wingo's contribution is affirmative, rather than merely critical. His aim is not to discredit liberalism, as though that were worth doing for its own sake. Perhaps more generously than we liberal thinkers deserve, he sets out to nurture themes in liberal thought that have been subdued, and to push a little into the background those jagged aspects of our political philosophy that we have tended stupidly to exaggerate. He seeks to enrich and contextualize our discussions of legitimacy, autonomy, justice, even transparency, and to make us ponder their significance. He does not seek simply to discredit them.

At the dawn of our tradition, we learned from Aristotle that the best political theory is the offspring of comparative politics; we see how to theorize our own politics when we make it strange to ourselves by comparing it to the politics of another society. Now, as I said, Ajume Wingo writes about the United States, and it is contemporary American liberalism that he is seeking to enrich. But he does so as an outsider, an African, a Cameroonian, of royal blood and considerable political experience. Those who remain inward-looking quickly learn to miss or blur the most interesting features of the politics of their own society. There is no chance of that with this book. We should be grateful to Ajume Wingo for teaching us to see things new and for showing us – in a way that many of us would do well to imitate – how the new things that we see can be incorporated into our reflection on the things that for too long have been dominating our vision.

New York
July 30, 2002

Acknowledgments

The satisfaction I take in having completed this book is like that of a gardener looking over his own small plot, seeing in its fruits his own labor and sweat and remembering not a few sleepless nights worrying over killing frosts, choking weeds, and withering droughts. But a gardener knows that the end of his labor depends on its beginnings; no amount of sweat and labor will yield a crop when the soil is barren, and no amount of restless tossing and turning in bed can help when the sun doesn't shine or the rain doesn't fall. In the course of writing *Veil Politics*, I've had the exceptionally good fortune of teachers, friends, and colleagues who have provided me with a fertile plot to work, helped me till and plant that plot, and pushed me to weed and nurture my ideas and arguments.

Two people deserve special mention for their role in the writing of this book. The first is Jeremy Waldron, whose kind encouragement so many years ago helped to germinate the first seeds of this book. He was the first person who listened to me talk about my ideas, and when he said "these are good ideas, stick to them," I heard and believed him. I can only hope that this book – in many ways the fruit borne of that first encouragement – adequately reflects how much his generosity and support have meant to me.

The second is Michael Kruse, a friend who stood by me from the beginning to the end of this project. He made valuable contributions to this book, reading each word of each draft, spending countless hours discussing, criticizing, and commenting on the arguments and ideas contained in this book. His critical eye forced me to think hard about – and sometimes, rethink entirely – many of the issues in the book, and while he reveled in playing devil's advocate with respect to the details, maintained an abiding faith in me and the project.

Acknowledgments

The first recognizable ancestor of this book was my doctoral dissertation at the University of Wisconsin–Madison, and my sincerest thanks go to the members of my committee for their support and encouragement: my advisor Patrick Riley, David Weberman, Paula Gottlieb, Yi-Fu Tuan, and Allen Buchanan. Since coming to Boston in 1997, I have been extremely fortunate to have access to some of the best minds in the field whose talents and abilities have been matched only by their generosity. Among these, I am especially grateful to Kwame Anthony Appiah and Kwasi Wiredu for the conversations we've had over the years on some of the ideas contained in this book. Thanks also to Jane Mansbridge, with whom I have had regular conversations on these issues, and my colleague Larry Blum, who read the entire manuscript and whose comments greatly improved Chapter 3. Sally Haslenger's comments on Chapter 2 were also very useful, as were comments, criticisms, and suggestions from Meira Levinson, David Lyons, Valeria Ottonello, Mary Sarko, Steven Teles, and Flavio Baroncelli, all of whom generously read all or parts of the manuscript. To Sanford Levinson, a friend with whom I share an interest in public monuments, I owe many thanks as well, not just for his input on the manuscript, but also for the opportunity to present parts of Chapter 3 at a seminar at the Law School at the University of Texas at Austin.

I am grateful to Neal Bruss and Larry Foster at the University of Massachusetts for helping me make a case for a reduced teaching load for a semester that gave me time to complete the book. The W. E. B. Du Bois Institute at Harvard, the Institute on Race and Social Division at Boston University, and the McCormack Institute of Public Affairs at the University of Massachusetts–Boston also provided invaluable assistance in the form of fellowships that allowed me access not only to the superb research facilities at these institutions, but more importantly to their phenomenal academic communities. In particular, Glenn Loury, the director of the Institute on Race and Social Division, has helped me tremendously by organizing forums that allowed me to present and discuss my ideas with others. During my tenure at the Institute, I spent countless hours with him, discussing ideas that have helped me both in the writing of this book and beyond, and his sharp mind was one of the most important forces that helped me hone and clarify my arguments.

The names of two of my most insightful critics are, alas, unknown to me, being the anonymous referees for Cambridge University Press. Their candid observations and suggestions helped me greatly to improve the organization and arguments in the text. Their thoughtful input has been but one part of the exemplary work Cambridge University Press has done in producing this book. To Douglas MacLean and Terence Moore (general series editor and general editor, respectively), I can only begin to express how grateful I am for their confidence in and support of this project from beginning to finish.

Finally, I would like to give a special acknowledgment to those who placed me on the path to this project. To Dennis O'Reilly, Janet Allen, Paul and Emy Gartzke, Elisabeth Bienert, Aaron Hyman, and Daniel Baker, I am especially grateful for the friendship and support they so freely offered to a newcomer to this country. To Bernard Williams, Janet Brougton, Samuel Scheffler, and John Searle, I offer heartfelt thanks for their inspiring example as teachers and wise instruction that first led me to political philosophy at the University of California, Berkeley.

Chapter 1

Introduction to Veil Politics

1.1. POLITICAL VEILS

One of the great monuments found in Washington, DC, is the Lincoln Memorial. Inscribed on the south wall of the monument is the text of the Gettysburg Address, above which is a mural depicting the angel of truth freeing a slave. Engraved on the north wall is the text of Lincoln's Second Inaugural speech. In the middle of the pavilion is the figure of Abraham Lincoln himself, his grave countenance casting a palpable aura over visitors.

The power of artifacts like the Lincoln Memorial to stir the emotions is quite remarkable. But they are not alone in having this power: Novels, plays, films, and even manipulative television advertisements and greeting cards have the same ability to tap into the emotions of spectators. What – if anything – distinguishes civic monuments from artifacts like these? Are monuments of this kind merely public art of a particular kind, or do they serve another function that distinguishes them from other kinds of art?

One way to see what distinguishes civic monuments is to look at their effects. As we might expect, one of the effects of civic memorials is aesthetic. Just as an innovative artwork may please the eye or make us look with new eyes by jarring our sensibilities with new forms and unexpected lines, the Lincoln Memorial appeals to classical standards of proportion and symmetry, while the Vietnam Memorial is startling with its stark simplicity. For many works of art, this aesthetic effect is *all* that is intended – this is art for art's own sake.

Memorials like the Lincoln and the Vietnam War memorials, however, also play a socializing role as well: They are devices that convey particular social, political, and moral values. The Lincoln Memorial, for

1

instance, is not just a piece of art in an imposing venue. From its stairs rising from the reflecting pool before it to the names of the members of the Union ringing it at the top, the Memorial is an amalgam of symbols that tell a story about the ideals of the United States of America. The statue of Lincoln, as it were, tirelessly delivers his civic lessons to citizens, ceaselessly asking citizens to prove worthy of the fallen in this society, and serving as a physical manifestation of Pericles's statement that "It is by honor, and not by gold, that the helpless end of life is cheered." Simply put, Lincoln is a paideia for the discipline of living alongside one another in this community. The civic lessons he silently delivers to the polity are more than any words that can flow from the lips of a living civic tutor.

This effect is, in part, the result of design; the classical motif and scale of the statue all strike predictable chords in Americans. But design is only partly responsible for the meaning that has been invested in the Memorial and the effect it has on many visitors. The other component is its own history, for the Lincoln Memorial is a living symbol, acquiring new significance as time passes. It is no accident that it was to the steps of the Lincoln Memorial that Martin Luther King, Jr., and other civil rights marchers were drawn during the March on Washington. In the process, they drew upon its significance as a symbol of the promise of America and the sacrifices made for their sake, and at the same time transformed the Memorial, making it a symbol both of the will of the disenfranchised and of entry into full citizenship.

The Lincoln Memorial is a particularly recognizable political symbol, but there are many other less obvious devices that serve similar socializing functions – flags, uniforms, anthems, and pantheons of civic heroes. Indeed, such symbols are present in every state. Where will one find a state in the world without cultural, ethic, or political heroes, without a flag, without a national anthem? These objects, like language, highways, and cars, are found in all states. But unlike highways, languages, and cars, whose functions are apparent, the various functions of things like numismatic symbols, flags, and national anthems may easily be overlooked or dismissed altogether as merely decorative.

Consider, for instance, a simple penny. Its function is most obviously to serve as a medium of exchange or a store of value. But at the same time it is adorned with symbols that are not obviously linked to that role. Incused on the head side is Lincoln's face, gaunt with the burdens of office. Behind the collar of the regalia is carved "Liberty"; a halo of "In God We Trust" adorns the head. On the tail side of the penny is a classic-style temple in which a sharp eye can make out the form of Lincoln himself. Above the memorial is a nimbus, "United States of America"; below, the motto of the United States, "E Pluribus Unum."

Why go to these lengths to adorn a penny? From a practical point of view, there are obvious virtues to using the faces of well-known figures on coins, currency, and stamps. Humans are very good at distinguishing human faces; using a famous figure's face on media of exchange is, then, an effective way of foiling counterfeiting efforts. But if *this* is the ultimate rationale for adding detail to money, what accounts for the particular images and details used? Other, more notorious historical figures (such as Napoleon Bonaparte or Adolph Hitler) are at least as familiar to most Americans as Lincoln – and are certainly more easily recognized than, say, Andrew Jackson, Alexander Hamilton, or Salmon P. Chase. If familiarity were the fundamental concern, why not place images of *these* persons on currency and coin? If the image of Elvis Presley is appropriate for a first-class stamp, why isn't it fitting for the dime or the ten dollar bill?

The reason it *isn't* is that the decisions we make about symbols of this kind are not just utilitarian ones, ones that turn on how easily an image can be forged or recognized. Rather, they also play an important role in shaping our political and moral intuitions; they are, in fact, often explicitly designed and selected with an eye toward valorizing particular images or individuals, all for the purpose of presenting, and thereby subtly upholding, the values and ideals associated with those images.

In this way, the image of Lincoln finds its way into every pocket and every child's piggybank, and in so doing, various ideals and virtues associated with the image of Lincoln find their way as well into the daily lives of citizens. In a sense, this image becomes invisible, blending as it does into the commonplace background of everyday life. But, like language and the countless other tacit assumptions of everyday life, these unobtrusive images play a role in shaping our values, judgments, and intuitions. Blaise Pascal noted that the best way to develop faith is to go live among the faithful. In a similar way, we might say that the best way to develop the habits, intuitions, and character of a citizen is to live amidst the symbols of a particular polity.

As an illustration of the power of these symbols, consider the way Lincoln's public image has been transformed since 1860. We live in a world in which Lincoln ranks with the founding fathers in greatness – perhaps surpassed only by Washington in importance. Today there is no controversy in citing Lincoln as an influence: In an important sense, the legacy of Lincoln is not one that American politicians today need explicitly to embrace, but is one of the "givens" of American politics. During his lifetime, however, and for a time even after his assassination, Lincoln was a deeply divisive political figure.[1] How does such a change come about?

In some respects, this swing from divisive to unifying figure is not so much the result of a change in the public's sensibilities as it has been a reshaping of Lincoln's image. That is, it isn't Lincoln the *man*, with all his complexities and paradoxes, who commands this authority. Rather, it is the iconic *representation* of Lincoln, the backwoods-railsplitter-turned-Great-Emancipator, that has been embraced virtually all along the political spectrum. Clearly, this representation fails to do justice to the complexities of the man; but at the same time, this simplification of the man has conveniently turned Lincoln into a common symbol, one that represents values and ideals that are part of the assumed background to politics in the United States.

This caricature of Lincoln functions as what I shall call a political veil. Real veils are cloth sheets that block a subject's direct perception of an object. *Political veils* – political symbols, rituals, mythologies, and traditions – serve the same kind of veiling function. But instead of standing between a perceiver and an object, these veils mediate between citizens and a political structure. Where ordinary veils smooth rough edges, mask wrinkles, and highlight a body's best features, political veils gloss over historical details or aspects of the political apparatus, offering instead an idealized image of the system or a stylized representation of a civic virtue.

Political veils, then, have a dual purpose. Obviously, they have the ability to *hide*, *distort*, or *misrepresent*. Thus, the popular images of the founding fathers typically obscure their foibles and suppress their mistakes to the point that they appear almost superhuman; instead of objective biography, we are given Parson Weems. But this capacity to *obscure* at the same time allows veils to *enhance* perception of the object by setting off its most attractive features. Ordinary frames, pedestals, and other adornments can help to bring an onlooker's attention to specific

---

[1] Lincoln's status is, of course, itself the product of history. For a discussion of the transformation of Lincoln from divisive figure to a kind of apolitical civic hero, see David Herbert Donald's "Getting Right with Lincoln," in *Lincoln Reconsidered: Essays on the Civil War Era*, 3rd edition (New York: Vintage Books, 1961).

4

features of an object. In the same way, a good caricature can often capture quite accurately the essence of a personality or a person's character, notwithstanding its omission of a mass of details.

Veils politics is a style of political practice that recognizes the force of veils and intentionally uses them for political purposes. As a style of political practice, veil politics is not wedded to any particular political content – one may self-consciously use veils for purposes democratic or authoritarian, liberal or totalitarian. Veil politics, then, can be thought of as a means of implementing a particular political system, making the degree to which a system intentionally uses veils – creating, manipulating, and modifying them – lie, as it were, on an axis orthogonal to the political spectrum.

Political veils, then, can be put to many different purposes, depending on the kind of state in which they are used. In a liberal democracy, for instance, they serve to highlight core liberal democratic values and the preferred core narratives of the polity. Through the images of moral and civic exemplars, drawn from mythic or highly idealized history and biography, members of a liberal democracy form affections for such values as respect for the law, civic participation, liberty, cohesion, and solidarity.

Veils are surely not the only way of impressing these values on people, for argument, debate, and deliberation certainly have important roles in this process as well. But veils give us an additional tool, and a particularly powerful one at that. For in the same way that a good caricature may reveal a person's character better than a full biography, fables and myths, dramatic imagery, and art may be far more effective in transmitting civic values and ideals than some more truthful or unadorned representation.

1.2. STRUCTURAL AND FUNCTIONAL FEATURES OF VEILS

To get a better idea of how veils help to instill and support civic values, let us take a closer look at the structure of political veils and the various functions they may serve. Structurally, all veiled objects have a *superficial image* and a *deep image* – the former is what first presents itself to the eye of the onlooker, the latter is the true nature of the object. While all veils share this basic form, their functions may vary considerably, depending on the nature of the veiling. The functions of political veils can (on analogy with the functions of real veils) be distinguished into three

5

basic types, corresponding to the nature and purpose of the superficial image.

1.2.1. *Veils as Aesthetic Adornment*

The most straightforward function of veils is to *cover* an object. In many cases, this covering function is used to deceive the viewer by presenting a wholly misleading image of the true nature of the object. But veils used simply as adornment may have a less duplicitous role as well, not to mislead but rather to draw attention to an object that, if presented in an unadorned way, would be overlooked or ignored.

The most obvious qualities used to draw attention are aesthetic ones – ones that appeal to judgments of beauty and aesthetic quality. Because these standards likely vary from place to place, the effectiveness of particular veils will depend on context; standards of beauty applicable in the Florentine Renaissance may be seen as grotesque or repellent by people at another place or time. Veils, then, are a kind of public art that serves a political purpose and is directed at a particular set of people shaped by a common set of customs.

Manipulation of an object's visual qualities may be the most obvious way of veiling, but it is not the only way of presenting an object or institution in a way that makes it more attractive to the public. The *story* or *history* associated with an object can have a similar effect. For instance, the important part of many museum-goers' experience is not the actual material of the artifacts they see, but the *history* of those objects. It is not *just* the beauty of the *Mona Lisa* – nor even the mysterious smile – that draws crowds of tourists, but the way this famous painting is bound up in the viewer's idea of history, culture, and her own place in relation to that history and culture. An insignificant-looking sonnet is seen in a new light once suspected of coming from the pen of Shakespeare; an otherwise worthless object rumored to have been a saint's, a hero's – even a villain's – suddenly acquires a special status.

Just as with appeals to culture-specific standards of beauty, one cannot expect persons who are not *already* steeped in the history and are not *already* well versed in the symbols of a culture to be moved by the political veils used in that culture. Present an average American with an African ceremonial mask displayed in a museum and she is liable to treat it as a purely aesthetic object. What is missing from her experience is an appreciation of the social function such an artifact plays in its own milieu – its role in the community, the values and practices that it connotes, the history and traditions that it evokes when used.[2]

In the same way, the experience of civic symbols in the United States – the White House, the Capitol, the Vietnam War Memorial, and others – is for many Americans not *just* an aesthetic one, nor is it one that is independent of their own particular context. Rather, it is an experience shaped by a whole cluster of social, historical, and political features; where someone unfamiliar with U.S. history sees only an impressive statue of Lincoln, another naturally brings to mind the Civil War, the emancipation of slaves, and the dramatic reworking of the United States polity that Lincoln has come to represent.

The associations that make this experience possible are not learned from books or classroom lectures. A citizen doesn't learn to be a patriot – to feel the swell of pride when, at a time of crisis or tragedy, she hears the national anthem or sees the flag – in the way she might memorize a list of dates or a set of multiplication tables. Instead, this process may be more accurately likened to language acquisition, in which citizens learn these associations not by explicit lessons, but by immersion in a complex symbolic milieu.

1.2.2. Veils as Temptations

As adornments, veils can help to make an otherwise unattractive or uninspiring institution or practice more palatable to citizens. Veils can also be used to add mystique to objects, drawing citizens in to investigate and to discover the deep image for themselves. For instance, the status of civil servant, citizen, or soldier may be invested with superficial qualities or significance that tempt people toward them, engaging their attention enough to reveal their more robust deep nature.

The power that veils have to hide aspects of an object or procedure can, then, also exert a powerful attraction. David Hume has noted the deep truth that:

'Tis certain nothing more powerfully animates any affection, than to conceal some part of its object by throwing it into a kind of shade, which at the same time that it shews enough to pre-possess us in favour of the object, leaves still some work for the imagination.[3]

---

[2] See Ajume H. Wingo, "African Art and the Aesthetics of Hiding and Revealing," *British Journal of Aesthetics*, Vol. 38, No. 3 (1998), pp. 251–64.
[3] David Hume, *A Treatise of Human Nature*, ed. L. A. Selby-Bigge (Oxford, UK: Clarendon Press, 1978), p. 422.

Writers, performers, and artists from Alfred Hitchcock to Gypsy Rose Lee all know the power of suggestion – that the best way to fire the imagination is to give the audience not the object itself, but the *hint* of it. When all is visible, nothing is left to the imagination. When only the silhouette and nothing more is given, the individual mind has room to work by itself on an object, endowing it with details of its own creation and drawing the individual in for a closer look.

A veil, in other words, can be characterized by what I have elsewhere called the *aesthetics of hiding and revealing*.[4] The surface attraction invites investigation, broadcasting the fact that there is something more than what is revealed, the deeper function. The outer surface stimulates the imagination, and by doing so, helps to support the practices veiled in this way.

1.2.3. *Veils as Idealizations*

One additional purpose that veils may serve is that of an idealization, a simplification of a complex object, practice, doctrine, or figure. The caricature of Lincoln discussed earlier is one such example, as are other stylized representations of civic figures and many popular versions of a state's history. Each elides many details and particulars that any literal account would have to reflect.

The virtue of this kind of simplification or idealization is that by blurring details, they also obscure possible points of conflict among citizens. The superficial image of Lincoln, for instance, is that of the president who preserved the Union and freed the slaves – an image that has come to be embraced by virtually everyone in the United States today. What this image leaves out are many of the more unattractive or controversial qualities of the man – the Lincoln who suspended writs of habeas corpus, who instituted an income tax and dramatically expanded the role of the federal government, whose Emancipation Proclamation freed only those slaves *outside* areas controlled by the Union Army.

This richer, more complex image of Lincoln may be more intellectually satisfying (and is certainly more veridical) than the two-dimensional version found in popular lore. But it should be acknowledged that for *political* purposes, this richer view would do little to help create a common symbol around which Americans of all political views can rally.

---

[4] For details, see Wingo, ibid.

Adding details simply adds potential points of conflict, and in their role of *obscuring* these sometimes divisive details, political veils help to eliminate some of those sources of disagreement.

1.2.4. One Veil, Multiple Functions

In the preceding sections, I have described three different ways that veils can be used to engage citizens and help to instill in those citizens particular values and ideals. It would be a mistake, however, to assume that any given veil can have only *one* of these functions. More typically, effective political veils will play multiple roles, depending on the individual experiencing them.

For instance, the superficial image of a veil may, by virtue of its aesthetic qualities alone, shape the behavior of casual observers in particular ways; in this case, it functions as an aesthetic adornment. At the same time, however, it may also (either through its aesthetic qualities or the mystique it generates) prompt some curious individuals to investigate the deep image behind the veil; for these individuals, the veil also functions as a temptation.

One risk of this deeper look is disenchantment – what the adorned surface appearance promises to the onlooker, the deep image fails to deliver. But it is also possible for this closer look to support the effect of the surface image, in which case those who penetrate the veil may come to have an even greater appreciation for the object than those guided simply by the superficial appearance. In this latter case, the veil functions as an idealization, a simplified representation that highlights particular features of the object it adorns, presenting those features as that object's more salient or essential qualities.

This ability of a single veil to have different functions makes veils a useful tool for supporting particular political values and ideals in a population in which people differ widely in their abilities and interests. That is, veils provide a means of targeting very different audiences – the casual onlooker and the more skeptical or reflective citizen – in a way that can engage both.

An interesting illustration of this use of veils is in Maimonides's *The Guide for the Perplexed*.[5] A philosopher and scholar of Judaism in the twelfth century, Maimonides was concerned with what I regard as a

---

[5] Moses Maimonides, *The Guide for the Perplexed*, Vol. 1, transl. by Shlomo Pines (Chicago: University of Chicago Press, 1963).

problem of political stability. Specifically, he anticipated that allowing details of the halakha (the part of the Torah concerned with the complexities of the norms of conduct and of religious beliefs) to be accessible to the general population would erode faith. According to Maimonides, the philosophical aptitude required to appreciate these issues correctly are not distributed evenly. Genuine philosophers, he believed, might be capable of sustaining their faith when faced with these complexities and controversies, but genuine philosophers are in short supply. To insist that everyone confront these issues would, then, be to impose a burden on the majority of people who do not want to live the life of contemplation and perhaps even to threaten the established social and political order.

And yet, according to Maimonides, the law is both the ultimate source of cohesion in the Jewish community and a well from which philosophers draw their inspiration for their lives of contemplation. Presenting the law, then, demands doing justice to both roles, without confusing the two. Maimonides's solution was to present the law in an equivocal way, in a manner that provides the practical guidance that the community requires while at the same time giving the philosopher material for thought and reflection. Indeed, he says of his own discussion,

That which is said about all this is in equivocal terms so that the multitude might comprehend them [the laws] in accord with the capacity of their understanding and the weakness of their representation, whereas the perfect man [i.e., the philosopher], who is already informed, will comprehend them otherwise.[6]

As I interpret this passage, Maimonides is attempting to make philosophy available to those with "able minds" while at the same time maintaining public faith in the laws that are necessary for the survival of the community of which the philosopher is a part. Thus, he writes:

A sage accordingly said that a saying uttered with a view to two meanings is like an apple of gold overlaid with silver filigree-work having very small holes . . . the external meaning ought to be as beautiful as silver, while the internal meaning ought to be more beautiful than the external one, the former being in comparison to the latter as gold is to silver. *Its external meaning ought to contain in it something that indicates to someone considering it what is to be found in its internal meaning, as happens in the case of an apple of gold overlaid with silver filigree-work having very small holes. When looked at from a distance or with imperfect attention, it is deemed to be an apple of silver; but when a full sighted observer looks at it with full attention,*

6 Ibid., p. 9, my emphasis.

its interior becomes clear to him and he knows that it is gold. The parables of the prophets . . . are similar. *Their external meaning contains wisdom that is useful in many respects, among which is the welfare of human societies, as is shown by the external meaning of [p]roverbs* [sic] *and of similar sayings. Their internal meaning, on the other hand, contains wisdom that is useful for beliefs concerned with the truth as is.*[7]

Maimonides's presentation of the law itself can be seen as a sort of veil with multiple functions. Its superficial image operates on those individuals whose capacities do not allow them to understand the complex "philosophical" aspects of the law, allowing them to sustain a stable and well-ordered community. At the same time, those who realize that the superficial image of the law is composed of mere parables, myths, or tradition will also see (by virtue of their philosophical training) the ultimate importance of those myths and traditions for sustaining the social and political order. While there is a danger that those who "see through" the veil will suffer disenchantment and lose faith, this deeper understanding – the recognition of the "gold" that underlies the "silver" surface – should ultimately *enhance* their faith in the laws.

In the preceding quotation, Maimonides captures some of the important possibilities of political veils. These veils are not intended to bar individuals from seeing through them, but neither are they intended to pull the unwilling into a deeper investigation of the law. Instead, they are designed to respond to whatever disposition individuals may have, and do so in ways that guide people of many different interests, backgrounds, and abilities to a common goal. Those individuals who are engaged in theoretical life (what Aristotle refers to as "the life of contemplation") will be able to penetrate the veils via these "holes." But obstacles should be set up so that only those whose faith will not be undermined by seeing the truth will be able to do so.[8]

1.3. VEIL POLITICS IN PRACTICE

As I have presented them, political veils work in a variety of way to support a political structure. To a certain extent, the effectiveness of veils depends on their being unobtrusive, blending into the background of

---

[7] Ibid., p. 12, my emphasis.
[8] This view of veiled objects as having a "double meaning" is echoed by Leo Strauss, who has a similar view of texts and histories as having two layers of meaning, with one accessible to the masses and the other open only to the "elites."

our ordinary lives in a way that makes the values they stand for part of what we take for granted.

Another important factor that contributes to their effectiveness is their forming an interlocking network or tapestry of symbols and images that, taken as a whole, reflect the virtues, principles, and ideals of the political structure. If one wants to see the role played by these liberal democratic veils, one shouldn't look at a patch here or a thread there (the Lincoln numismatic symbol, for example). The full effect comes to light only when one takes the mass of discrete symbols – the sacred civic spaces, hallowed buildings such as the White House and the Capitol, and sacrosanct objects like the American flag – as a whole. Only then can one begin to feel the weight of veils and start to appreciate the extent to which political symbols appear all around us.

The basic function I am claiming for political veils is to serve as a means of effectively embedding the polity's values in the lives of citizens until the values of that polity are second nature to them. Like argumentation and open debate of issues, veils are a special way of inviting people to reflect upon proposals and to take action. Like rational political debate, the end of veils is action or behavior of a particular kind; their purpose is to persuade citizens to take those actions, to behave in the requisite way. Unlike argumentation, however, veils bypass the explicit use of rational faculties, instead appealing to symbols and images that have been invested with meaning and emotional significance to shape the actions, habits, and character of citizens.

Thinking in terms of veils and being attuned to their effect on the basic character of citizens lends considerable importance to what otherwise might seem to be purely ceremonial gestures or rhetorical flourishes. For instance, recall the heated debate and deliberation concerning the design of the FDR Memorial in Washington, D.C., and the passionate arguments surrounding the construction of a World War II Memorial on the Mall. Can mere differences in aesthetic judgments account for the passions that these debates elicit? Or is there something more at stake in these arguments?

Recall also how Martin Luther King, Jr., and the civil rights marchers waved American flags and sang patriotic songs as they marched to the steps of the Lincoln Memorial in Washington, D.C. There, in his "I Have a Dream" speech, King called on living Americans to honor the promises made by their own civic heroes who founded this nation by accepting African Americans as full citizens in the nation of their birth. King's claim for social and political justice had no need of this location or his eloquent oratory for its justification. But it did need those trappings to be heard by the rest of America.

Opening our eyes to the veils that surround us everyday, it becomes clear that the business of making, manipulating, and modifying veils is hardly new. It is as old as the idea that to motivate people to action, one must appeal to things familiar and dear to them – their customs, their traditions, their image of themselves. *Political myths*, for instance, have long been acknowledged to have instrumental value in mobilizing people to action. These myths do not merely entertain – although good myths surely do that. They also have a didactic function, teaching lessons of virtue, morals, and character.

Classical mythology can be read as a rich study of general human psychology that embeds deep truths about human nature in an entertaining and vivid story. In much the same way, political myths function as veils embedding the values and purposes of a community in stories that can engage even the least civic-minded citizens. Myths typically present the origins of a society in ways that flatter the people who live in it, representing their community as part of a divine plan or as the legacy of a hardy, virtuous race of heroes who tamed the wild frontier. As fabricated stories of a community's beginnings, however, these tales actually speak to that society's end – its aims, values, and purposes.

Political symbols are another kind of veil. These provide ways to objectify myths or stand in for particular persons or institutions. In this role of "placeholder," the symbol often comes to be treated not merely as a mark, but as much more: People begin to associate it with objects or narratives that appear with it. Further, the way political symbols are deployed or used alters their own significance as well as that of others. Sometimes this amounts to "transferring" feelings associated with it to other things, as happens when a struggling politician figuratively wraps herself in the flag; at other times this path is reversed, and a previously insignificant symbol acquires meaning merely by its association with an event or figure. Such symbols have no fixed, invariant meaning but rather can take on different ones at different times, depending on the variety of situations within which they are used.

Political rhetoric is another device that functions as a kind of veil. Great orations are more than the text on the page or teleprompter, and their greatness depends not just on the argument being made, but on the way the argument is presented. The art of oratory is that of drawing on familiar themes, structures, and symbols, using the invested significance of those elements either to engage the audience or to reshape the meanings of those elements themselves to make the audience think in new ways about old issues. Like other political veils, however, effective political rhetoric overlays the content of a speech with a façade, one that may either obscure the true content or serve as a more effective "delivery device" than unadorned speech.[9]

Political rituals constitute yet another class of political veils. As characterized by David Kertzer, rituals of this kind are actions performed by people within a political unit; these actions are "highly structured, standardized sequences and [are] often enacted at certain places and times that are themselves endowed with special symbolic meaning."[10] Rituals in general (not just political ones) owe much of their power to the fact that as repetitions, they quickly work their way into the routine patterns of everyday life. Political rituals exploit this to good effect, often centering on the reenactment of some mythic event, such as the celebration of the "birth of a country" or what is popularly known in the West as an "Independence Day." Other rituals include the singing of patriotic songs such as the national anthem at sporting events and the ceremonial trappings of inaugurations. Parades celebrating national holidays, the protocol surrounding state visits, the pomp and circumstance of presidential inaugurations, parliamentary practices – all belong to the long list of rituals and symbols that exist in liberal democratic societies.

Finally, I note that certain kinds of *civic pedagogy* are closely related to the practice of veil politics; this is a topic I explore in much greater detail in Chapter 5.[11] For now, I will simply note that the purpose of civic education is to "align" the aims and values of children – future full members of the state – with the state's fundamental political values. By transmitting these values from one generation to the next, a program of civic education can be thought of as a way of *reproducing* the state.

As I will argue in Chapter 5, one effective means of doing this is to develop dispositions to respond in specific ways to particular symbols or ideas, and then to forge a link between those symbols and the values

---

[9] I do not mean to suggest that *all* political speeches are veiled in this way. In many contexts, rhetorical flourishes would be counterproductive. That said, however, it should also be noted that the image of the plain-spoken, almost inarticulate "man of the people" is often just another type of veil: a public representation of guileless virtue.

[10] David I. Kertzer, *Ritual, Politics and Power* (New Haven, CT: Yale University Press, 1988), p. 9.

[11] Note that civic pedagogy does intertwine with tradition; however, I will discuss it separately for reasons that will become clear in Chapter 5.

of interest. Such a program of civic pedagogy that uses veils is, I will argue, of great value in a liberal democracy, since it gives us a way to engender the central civic values of a liberal democracy without having to resort to coercion.

1.4. VEILS AND LIBERALISM – AN ESSENTIAL TENSION?

As I have characterized them, political veils appeal to emotional and aesthetic reactions to initiate, strengthen, and enhance feelings such as solidarity, pride, and reverence.

Veils are also what I call *conceptually ambiguous*, in the sense that different persons may have similar overt reactions to a single veil, yet have very different thoughts about it. The woman facing the flag and singing the national anthem next to me at the start of a baseball game may have beliefs about what that flag and anthem – and the country they represent – stand for that are very different from my own. Yet singing together and honoring the same flag brings the two of us together in an important way. These common symbols are, as it were, vessels that we can share while still filling them with very different contents. This ambiguity allows diverse people to have a common emotional or behavioral reaction to the veil despite their dramatically different beliefs and desires.[12]

Veils, then, are a means of persuasion that, in an important sense, circumvent rational faculties. They are, if not necessarily malicious deceptions and manipulation, at least something less than the truth, playing more to habits, emotions, and intuitions than to reason. They are pictures or images that foster a particular way of looking at and living in the world. Residing in the non-rational realm, they have a nature that is difficult to capture in the philosopher's usual categories of rationality and irrationality, and next to impossible to govern with the inflexible laws of logic.

As such, an obvious objection to the use of veils in a liberal democracy is that it is a threat to autonomy and self-determination. After all, it seems

---

[12] For a discussion of the differences between the emotive and the conceptual meanings of concepts, see C. L. Stevenson, "Persuasive Definitions," *Mind*, Vol. 47, No. 187 (July, 1938), p. 331. See also Jeremy Waldron's "Indirect Discrimination," in *Equality and Discrimination: Essays in Freedom and Justice*, eds. Stephan Guest and Alan Milne (Philadelphia, PA: Coronet Books, 1985), pp. 93–100.

that the very legitimacy of the liberal state and its powers rests on the consent of individuals endowed with reason and the ability to scrutinize the status quo with a critical eye. Intentional efforts to play to the non-rational aspects of citizens, be it through subtle rhetorical methods or blatant appeals to fear and jealousy, violate at least the spirit of liberal democracy.

The threat posed by veils to the principles of liberal democracy is quite real, for mythic narratives have long been used for highly illiberal purposes. European kings and their descendants, for example, attempted to justify their rule by appealing to myths of divine authority. Since their rule depended on their subjects (and perhaps even themselves) believing this myth, it had to be impenetrable. In terms of veils, this story of origins had to be opaque, one that could hide completely the facts that lay beyond it.

Opacity politics is a particular version of veil politics, one that employs methods aimed at deceiving the public by replacing harsh, unpalatable realities with more acceptable images. Thus, the absolute power wielded by the tyrant is presented as the natural authority due to the hand-picked temporal representative of the gods, *not* as the result of a combination of brutal opportunism and historical accident. The monarch commands allegiance by being chosen by God to lead, *not* because he can crush opposition. In these cases, the purpose of these opaque facades is to mask facts because they are too awful to stand the light of the day; they hide these facts because revealing them would be a direct threat to the political structure.

In extreme cases, it may be that the myth is essential to the state, and debunking it would knock the foundations out from under the whole political structure. This may have been the case in Imperial Japan, where the belief in the divine nature of the Emperor was a key element underlying his (and the government's) authority. A perhaps less extreme case is that of the lies that the U.S. government told the public during the Vietnam War about the number of casualties and the progress of the war. When these were revealed as lies, it was natural for citizens to doubt the sincerity of the entire governmental apparatus.

1.4.1. Opacity and Transparency Politics

Using veils to hide that which is too awful to show constitutes a special case of veil politics, one that I shall call *opacity politics*. Like veil politics in general, opacity politics is a style of political practice that makes intentional use of veils for political purposes. What distinguishes this style from the more general concept of veil politics is that opacity politics is explicitly concerned with the deployment of impenetrable veils, ones that are designed and employed in a way that resists efforts to see through those veils.

The Enlightenment appeal to rational consent can be seen as an attempt to avoid the abuses of these opaque veils. Roughly, the approach sought to make the structure and workings of political institutions transparent to individuals. With nothing to obscure the true nature of the political system, consent to that system could be turned into a means of legitimizing the system.

The importance of transparency in politics runs throughout the history of liberalism. The main aim of John Locke's work in the *First Treatise of Government* was to expose the duplicity of Sir Robert Filmer's arguments supporting the British Crown, tear down the obscuring trappings of political power, and replace it with a rational justification of legitimate, consensual government. For Locke, the ultimate basis of the legitimacy of a political system lies in the consent of those living within it. Pleasing but deceptive images might prove effective means of manipulating the public, but by Lockean standards they are quite incompatible with the legitimacy of any state that would use them.

Locke's project is a particular example of what I call *transparency politics*. This is the alternative to veil politics, and is a style of political practice that seeks to minimize (or eliminate altogether) barriers between the public and the machinery of political institutions.

1.4.2. Reason and Transparency

The Lockean tradition of political thought focuses on political action as determined by the decisions of rational, deliberative, and self-interested persons. What is striking about this tradition is that it treats rationality as not just a way of justifying actions, but of explaining them as well. That is, for Locke, a person is first and foremost a rational agent; as such, to the extent that the person's actions are rational, those actions require no other explanation: Rational action is the norm; only irrational action requires further explanation.

From this perspective, the political practices that existed prior to the Enlightenment were seen as highly irrational, the result of opaque traditions and customs that deflected political affairs from their natural (rational) course. By stripping away these opaque veils, transparency politics was intended to create the conditions required for legitimate government. More than that, however, it was thought that the mere fact of transparency would be sufficient to cause individuals to act in ways that would promote autonomy, liberty, and respect for individuals. By allowing the public free and complete access to the facts, transparency politics would put rationality in command of politics, which would then quite naturally lead to the appropriate political arrangements.

This "politics of rationality" emerged most vividly during the French Revolution, with ideologues putting into practice the philosophical principle that the legitimacy of a government requires the rational participation of all citizens. They dismantled the ancient regime along with its symbols and traditions in favor of a new rational beginning.

Proponents of the French Revolution felt strongly that a justification for the state based on tradition and myth would lead to a state populated with passive citizens who blindly follow authority. Thus, it was argued that the demystification of the political tradition was necessary for the proper functioning of government. According to one of the leaders of the French Revolution, Maximilien Robespierre, demystification was necessary for the just and legitimate functioning of a democratic polity, for with demystification "all fictions disappear before truth, and follies collapse before reason, without compulsion, without persecution."[13]

The French Revolution, of course, succumbed to its own excesses. However, what survived in liberalism was a rejection of rule built on public deception, a view that lives on in John Rawls's characterization of what he refers to as "public reason" in his well-ordered society. Allowing public reason to operate, Rawls claims, requires that the basic structure of society should be "a public system of rules":

Thus the general awareness of their universal acceptance should have desirable effects and support the stability of social cooperation. . . .

Conceptions that might work out well enough if understood and followed by a few or even by all, so long as this fact were not widely known, are excluded by the publicity condition.[14]

---

[13] George Rude, *Robespierre* (Englewood Cliffs, NJ: Prentice Hall, 1967), p. 15. More generally, the use of veils for political purposes apparently threatens any system (liberal or otherwise) that takes *reason* to be sovereign – a point not lost on Plato, who was careful to ban poets in *The Republic*.

[14] John Rawls, *A Theory of Justice* (Cambridge, MA: Harvard University Press, 1971), pp. 55–6. For arguments on this point, see Samuel Scheffler, *The Rejection of Consequentialism* (Oxford, UK: Clarendon Press, 1982), pp. 43–51.

Insofar as veil politics would *allow* access to information of this sort to be limited, it seems clear that the practice of veil politics is fundamentally at odds with the principles of liberalism.

1.5. VEIL POLITICS IN POLITICAL PHILOSOPHY

What this attitude about veils represents is a particularly stubborn intuition: that liberal ideals are intimately linked to transparency, which in turn implies that there must be a conflict between liberal political ideals and the practice of veil politics. The deep question of the compatibility between liberalism and the purposeful use of veils is the focus of Chapter 3. Here, I want to describe how the issue of the legitimate use of veils is really part of a running debate over the place of devices like veils in political philosophy. At the heart of this debate is an essential tension that arises when we try to answer two different questions:

1. How do we create and sustain a stable political structure?
2. What legitimizes or justifies such a political structure?

The first of these can be seen as a question regarding political practice. The importance of this issue can be seen when we consider the very real problems that arise in efforts to import liberal democracy to parts of the developing world that have no preexisting democratic traditions.

For example, participation is a key element in any successful, thriving liberal democracy: A democracy is a state in which the citizens themselves sustain the political order. It is essential for the long-term survival of such a state that citizens actively participate in their own governing, even when it is not obvious that doing so is in their own benefit. Given this, it is important that there be some way to impress on citizens the value of participation.

In contrast, the second of these questions is a traditional problem for political philosophy: How do we justify the use of a particular set of political arrangements and institutions? What is the best way for us to live together? These questions are not concerned with the practical *implementation* of any particular political regime, but only the problem of determining which regime (or regimes) is justified.

Questions of justification and implementation generate tensions due to the fact that for at least some political arrangements, the answer to one appears to conflict with the answer to the other. This is particularly acute for the liberal, in that the means used by the most successful practitioners of political arts – including everyone from Machiavelli to bosses of modern political machines – are seldom ones that a principled liberal would be likely to endorse. Yet any political philosophy that hopes to have practical value must find a way to answer both of these questions: We might say (to appropriate a phrase from Kant) that *justification without motivation is empty, motivation without justification is blind*.

There are two general approaches to answering these two questions. What I call *pre-Enlightenment approaches* openly embrace the use of tradition, symbols, and myth as an answer to (1).[15] The hierarchical or organic political structure often embraced by pre-Enlightenment thinkers had the same basic organization as other familiar structures (such as that of the family or tribe). This fact gave them considerable power to mobilize support among citizens. At the same time, however, these thinkers often saw these structures as forming a normative ideal for government, which meant that adopting them solved not only the problem of motivation, but also that of justification.

A different solution is offered by what I call *post-Enlightenment approaches*. Post-Enlightenment-based politics purported to cut through the contextual basis of pre-Enlightenment political theory to a set of "first principles" derived from the essentially rational nature of persons. Persons were conceived of as having a common, rational nature that transcended specific cultural contexts, and it was this universal character of persons that would become the basis of legitimacy for liberal democratic political systems. Once formulated, these "first principles" could underwrite other more specific claims about politics and be used to explain other political and social phenomena.

The method of post-Enlightenment politics is characterized by abstract "system building." Instead of theorizing "from the ground up" by focusing on actual political phenomena and then constructing low-level political generalizations, post-Enlightenment politics posited high-level principles of human nature and rationality as axioms and derived from them political principles and generalizations.

Like the pre-Enlightenment tradition, this account also assumes that the two questions have a single answer. Here, however, the question about *justification* takes precedence. That is, the legitimacy of the political

[15] The term "pre-Enlightenment" here (and "post-Enlightenment" subsequently) refers to a style of or general approach to political philosophy, not a historical era. In this sense, contemporary communitarian accounts may be conceived of as part of the pre-Enlightenment tradition, despite their occurring *after* the Enlightenment, while the links forged by seventeenth century political thinkers between "right reason" and natural law harken back to Thomas Aquinas.

order is taken to lie in the consent of a rational agent. From there, the answer to (1) assumes that rational agents will, in the absence of external constraints, naturally be moved by their reason to act in accordance with the justified political principles.

Despite the significant differences between pre- and post-Enlightenment approaches (both with respect to the role of reason and the content of their political principles), they share important similarities as well. Perhaps most striking is the fact that each tradition faces the same basic problem of instilling and maintaining a set of core civic values needed to preserve the stability of the state. With respect to the problem of supporting and maintaining these common political values, thinkers as distinct as Burke and Robespierre can be seen as pursuing the same end with different means. For Burke, the way to support these values was by way of fictions, while for Robespierre, these same values were thought to be the result of citizens' use of reason and the availability of the relevant facts.

In an important sense, then, the fundamental difference between pre- and post-Enlightenment political thought comes not in what they aim to do, but in their respective conceptions of what drives human action. The post-Enlightenment theorist assumes that a person's mind is ultimately governed by reason, believing, as Michael Oakshott explained, the mind to be:

free from any obligation save the authority of reason . . . free from the influences of atmosphere, seasons, and temperature, a fully unencumbered mind that is free from prejudice and its relics, habit. He [the post-Enlightenment theorist] believes that the unhindered human "reason" (if only it can be brought to bear) is an infallible guide in political activity.[16]

This assumption differs from that of the pre-Enlightenment theorist, who asserts that one's character is largely defined by a particular social context. Each political tradition, then, makes assumptions regarding the source of the content of a person's character: Post-Enlightenment theorists focus on a fixed, *essentially rational* nature, while pre-Enlightenment theorists might be seen as committed to an *anti-essentialist* view of political subjects.

It is against this background that one can begin to understand why Burke would be troubled so much by the efforts of French

---

[16] Michael Oakeshott, *Rationalism in Politics* (Indianapolis, IN: Liberty Press, 1962), p. 7.

Revolutionaries who were prepared to go to such lengths to institute a radically rationalized regime:

> But now all is to be changed. All the pleasing illusion, which made power gentle and obedience liberal, which harmonized the different shades of life, and which, by a bland assimilation, incorporates with politics the sentiments which beautify and soften society, are to be dissolved by this new conquering empire of light and reason. All the decent drapery of life is to be rudely torn off. All the superadded ideas, furnished from the wardrobe of a moral imagination, which the heart owns, and the understanding ratifies, as necessary to cover the defects of our naked, shivering nature, and to raise it to dignity in our own estimation, are to be exploded as a ridiculous, absurd, and antiquated fashion.
>
> In this scheme of things, a King is but a man, a Queen is but a woman; a woman is but an animal, and an animal not of the highest order.[17]

Burke's concern here is not simply for the "decent drapery of life," nor is it merely a kind of slavish devotion to the past for its own sake. It is, instead, the worry of a man who sees this revolution as rejecting those features of government that allow it to function without having always to turn to coercion when reason fails. Burke realized what Robespierre did not – that "pleasing illusion" and "the decent drapery of life" are not features of just oppressive and unjust states. Rather, these are important elements of any political order that has a hope of surviving without succumbing to naked force.

In this book, I will challenge the presumption that the rationalist approach to political theory normally associated with liberalism can explain how fundamental political values such as stability, liberty, and cohesion needed for the reproduction of the state are generated and sustained. In doing so, I will argue that while rationality is a sine qua non of liberal democracy, its power is also sharply limited. Grounding government on the free consent of the governed is a central aim of any liberal state, and to the extent that transparency helps to secure this free consent, it has an obvious attraction for the liberal. However, there is a cost to being committed to transparency as a matter of principle, since that requires foregoing the opportunity of using political veils in a systematic and intentional way. It is, after all, reasonable to think that the widespread use of veils is due to their effectiveness, and that they

---

[17] Edmund Burke, *Reflections on Revolution in France*, ed. Thomas H. D. Mahoney (Indianapolis, IN: Bobbs-Merrill, 1955), p. 99.

would be powerful tools for liberal democrats – if only they could use them.

Rejecting (in principle if not in practice) the conscious use of veils, the modern liberal must rely on reason to sustain the state. In Chapter 2, however, I argue that there is no clear path from reason to liberal democracy, and that eschewing the use of veils leaves the future prospects of liberalism to chance.

For the time being, I will simply observe that we should never have expected reason to carry the load of motivating persons. That is, once we recognize the pervasive presence of veils and their influence on our everyday lives within a liberal democracy, we can see that what distinguishes liberal democracy from pre-Enlightenment political structures is not that liberalism rejects myth in favor of reason, but that it uses *different* myths for different purposes. Liberalism, then, does not represent *liberation* from tradition and myth but rather a *transformation* of them within a new political arrangement.

1.6. CONCLUSION

> "When I use a word," Humpty Dumpty said, in rather a scornful tone, "it means just what I choose it to mean – neither more nor less."
> The question is," said Alice, "whether you can make words mean so many different things." "The question is," said Humpty Dumpty, "which is to be master – that's all."
> Lewis Carroll, *Through the Looking Glass*[18]

Between political practice and political philosophy is the tension between concerns for effectiveness and legitimacy. Resolving this tension as it arises for liberal democracy is one of the general themes of this book. My approach to this problem is guided by two main principles. The first of these maintains that the questions of how states govern effectively and how they establish their legitimacy are distinct – that the optimal answer to one may *not* be optimal for the other. Therefore, it is not enough for us to find an answer to one and then simply assume that it will suffice for the other. Instead, we must critically assess proposals in terms of each of these questions individually.

[18] Lewis Carroll, *Through the Looking Glass* (New York: Puffin Books, 1994), p. 87.

The second of these principles is that the establishment and support of liberal democracy is too valuable to leave to chance. As I will argue in Chapter 2, reason alone cannot be counted on to instill and sustain the values needed for liberal democracy. Left on their own, individuals differ on too many premises for reason to lead to a single desired conclusion about issues as controversial as fundamental political values; and further, even if they would converge to a single cluster of values, it would be an astonishing coincidence if that happened to be a set of *liberal* values.

What veil politics offers is a way to support these basic values without having to rely on either reason or chance. Appealing to the meaning and cultural cache of traditional symbols and conventions in the service of liberal political values, then, is a way to avoid relying on the conclusions of individual reason, which may be as varied as the premises on which they are based. With Burke (although for rather different reasons), we can say that

We are afraid to put men to live and trade each on his own private stock of reason; because we suspect that the stock in each man is small, and that individuals would do better to avail themselves of the general bank and capital of nations and of ages.[19]

My principal aim is to show how we can use techniques that are neutral with respect to liberalism for liberal purposes. As I shall argue in Chapter 3, veils are an important kind of neutral technique; as a tool, they may be subject to abuse, but I believe that they are also capable of serving as powerful weapons *for* liberal democracy.

The arguments that follow are not intended to undermine the liberal's commitment to rationality. On the contrary, these arguments should be read as strengthening this commitment, but subject to one condition: that we recognize the *limitations* of rationality in generating and sustaining the core values of liberalism. As I have suggested in this chapter, modern liberals have typically failed to recognize the importance (indeed, the necessity) of the non-rational aspects of politics. The danger of this is that by ignoring the effects of the non-rational forces acting on us, we risk being ruled completely by them.

---

[19] Edmund Burke, *Reflections on the Revolution in France*, p. 87.

Chapter 2

History, Culture, and Persons

The Gettysburg Address stands as a marvelous example of oratory – perhaps unequaled in all of U.S. political history:

Four score and seven years ago our fathers brought forth on this continent, a new nation, conceived in liberty, and dedicated to the proposition that all men are created equal.

Now we are engaged in a great civil war, testing whether that nation, or any nation so conceived and so dedicated, can long endure.... We here highly resolve that these dead should not have died in vain – that this nation, under God, shall have a new birth of freedom – and that government of the people, by the people, for the people, shall not perish from the earth.

Saying precisely what Lincoln's *aims* were in his Address is a controversial historical question. Characterizing the *means* he employed and the lasting effects of the Address, however, is far less controversial. These means included the skillful use of the history, symbols, and rituals shared not just by Lincoln's immediate audience, but also by Americans on both sides of a war that threatened to tear the Union in two. On the face of things, Lincoln's purpose at Gettysburg was simple: to dedicate a cemetery to the Union's fallen dead. But the way he did this had much greater effects, for what at first appeared only as the dedication of a particular plot of land ended up having a decisive impact on how Americans conceive of themselves.

One reason for Lincoln's success in doing this derives from the occasion of his speech, which allowed him to draw on the long tradition of using funeral orations for political purposes, a tradition that stretched back more than twenty-five centuries to Pericles, whose own oration helped to shore up Athenian democracy following its defeat in the Peloponnesian War. As Pericles told his fellow citizens:

> I make the ancestors my opening theme, since it is right, it is appropriate here, to pay them memory's tribute. They, who dwelt nowhere but here, passed this land down to us, generation by generation, kept free by their valor. . . .
>
> Our political arrangement cannot be measured in contest with any other city's since we set the pattern rather than imitate them. By title we are a democracy, since the many, not just a few, participate in governing, and citizens are equal in their legal dealings with each other.[1]

Thirty years before the start of the Civil War, Chief Justice Story echoed Pericles's theme as he dedicated the Mount Auburn cemetery in Cambridge, MA. Stressing the role of these monuments to the dead as valuable schools for the living, he said:

> Our cemeteries, rightly selected and properly arranged, may be made subservient to some of the highest purposes of religion and human duty. They may preach lessons to which none may refuse to listen and which all that live must hear. Truth may be there felt and taught, in the silence of our own meditations, more persuasive and more enduring than ever flowed from human lips.[2]

The burial of the Athenian dead after a humiliating defeat was, through Pericles's eloquence, transformed into a powerful symbol of the vitality of Athenian democracy. In the same way, the cemetery at Gettysburg was transfigured by Lincoln from the site of a bitter internal struggle that threatened to destroy the Union into a common symbol for the *renewal* of that same polity.

In fewer than three hundred words, Lincoln put forth a radically new view of the origins and purposes of the Union that did much to change both the meaning of the war and the course of the nation that emerged from that conflict. One might think that such a shift in the foundations of the state would merit an intellectual debate. Lincoln's move, however, was instead an eloquent piece of rhetoric in which he pushed his vision by skillfully manipulating symbols and images – veils – that were invested with a meaning and significance that extended well beyond their place in historical and legal scholarship.

---

[1] Quoted in Garry Wills, *Lincoln at Gettysburg: The Words That Remade America* (New York: Simon and Schuster, 1992), pp. 249–50.

[2] Quoted in Garry Wills, *Lincoln at Gettysburg: The Words That Remade America* (New York: Simon and Schuster, 1992), p. 65.

Instead of engaging in a scholarly analysis of constitutional theory, Lincoln presented his own view of American history that made equality *the* central American value. That view was, in Lincoln's day, highly controversial and certainly capable of sustaining a long and drawn-out philosophical debate. Lincoln, however, offered no debate, but instead used his marvelous rhetorical skills to make America see these documents in a new and radically different way.

Lincoln's strategy was to redefine the public image of America's two principal documents, the Declaration of Independence and the Constitution. These two documents had already become powerful symbols for Americans, and Lincoln used this fact for a dramatic effect, employing the Declaration of Independence, a symbol long familiar to Americans, both to give a meaning to the events of the day and to impress a purpose on the Civil War – a purpose that was traced to the moment of the nation's founding. That "all men are created" equal may be a "self-evident truth" for many today, but in 1863, in a country in the midst of a terrible civil war over slavery, it was obvious that not everyone thought this way. Lincoln understood this, and understood as well that he could use this occasion with all its rich symbolism to tell a new version of American history that took seriously this statement of equality.

In this new version of American history, the Constitution was no longer an agreement entered into by states – which, presumably, could then opt out of the agreement as those in the Confederacy insisted they could. Instead, the Union was represented as the product of the Declaration. As a result, not only did the Union *predate* the individual states (thereby denying any the right to secede), but its purpose was also defined in that document. Lincoln had expressed this belief earlier in his political career, saying:

The expression of that principle [democracy] in our Declaration of Independence ... was the word *"fitly spoken"* which has proven an "apple of gold" to us. The *Union* and the *Constitution* are the *picture* of the *silver*, subsequently framed around it. The picture was made, not to *conceal* or *destroy* the apple; but to *adorn*, and *preserve* it. The *picture* was made for the apple – not the apple for the picture. So let us act, that neither picture, [n]or *apple* shall ever be blurred, bruised or broken.[3]

---

[3] Quoted in George P. Fletcher, *Our Secret Constitution* (New York: Oxford University Press, 2001), p. 68. The original of this metaphor is in Proverbs 25:11: "a word fitly spoken is like apples of gold in a setting of silver."

The genius of Lincoln's Address was his ability to convert what was indeed a radical political vision into common sense, a view that subsequent generations have come to take for granted. And he did this by harnessing his new political message to veils – histories, symbols, rituals, and customs already in place.[4]

Lincoln's actions did not go unnoticed. The *Chicago Times* editorialized:

It was to uphold this constitution, and the union created by it, that our officers and soldiers gave their lives at Gettysburg. How dare he, then, standing on their graves, misstate the cause for which they died, and libel the statesmen who founded the government? They were men possessing too much self-respect to declare that Negroes were equal, or were entitled to equal privileges.[5]

In an obvious sense, this editorial is illiberal, denying equality to African Americans. But in quite another sense, the *Times* perhaps saw Lincoln clearest of all, and voiced the concerns that a principled liberal would have with respect to his *methods*, if not his *intentions*.

What might be seen as objectionable about Lincoln's methods from a liberal point of view is that his powerful rhetoric largely bypasses rational deliberation. One reason for the liberal's discomfort with veils lies in a deeply held conception of the nature of persons as rational, autonomous agents. The intimate relationship between the conception of a person and judgments about legitimate political institutions and methods is to be expected: Any workable political theory must be predicated on some view of what humans are like even if this means assuming their nature axiomatically and working forward, or observing the behavior, desires, and aspirations of humans in the polity and moving backward to a conception of human life. The question, then, is how should we conceive of a political person?

---

[4] In section 4.3, I discuss Lincoln's manipulation of political veils in much greater detail. Here, I am focusing on showing the surprising extent to which rhetoric, rather than reason, has affected the course of political change and democratization. This can be seen in many other situations as well, including Martin Luther King, Jr.'s "I Have A Dream" speech. As a well-educated man with a doctoral degree, King was fully capable of engaging in a protracted intellectual debate. His speech, however, was obviously meant to harness the emotions of his listeners at least as much as it was designed to engage their reason.

[5] "The President at Gettysburg," *Chicago Times*, November 23, 1863 (quoted in Herbert Mitgang ed., *Abraham Lincoln: A Press Portrait*, Athens, GA: University of Georgia Press, 1994, p. 361).

2.1. PERSONS AND CULTURAL CONTEXTS

Properly conceived, the term "person" is a forensic term, distinct from any kind of biological classificatory structure. But if one's *personhood* is not determined by one's *being human*, what *does* determine it? One view common to many different philosophical accounts is what I call an *essentialist* conception of persons. Personhood, on this view, depends on having a common nature; the dramatic differences found between different cultures and societies are irrelevant to one's status as a person as long as one has that special nature. In the West, the quality often deemed essential to persons is related to self-consciousness or, more specifically, an agent's rationality or capacity to use reason.

In contrast, a *non-essentialist* conception maintains that the nature of persons is context- or culture-specific, and capable of being shaped by what I have called veils – customs, traditions, myths, rituals, and symbols. Veil politics is a method designed to exploit the possibility implicit in this non-essentialist view that veils can be used to align the political ambitions, aspirations, and goals of citizens in a non-coercive way.

While I am interested in the contrast between these two views of personhood, I am not concerned with resolving the question of which of these two accounts is the literally correct description. Rather, I am interested in the practical effect that each of these accounts has on the way we represent and reason about political agents. For instance, one of the practical effects of the essentialist view is to suggest that we use a "thin" conception of persons when making judgments about the nature of political institutions and legitimacy. Instead of representing individuals with all their emotional, cultural, and social idiosyncrasies, we should think of them in terms of what is essential to them as persons, that is, their rationality. In contrast, the non-essentialist account suggests a "thicker" view of persons, one that treats context-specific properties as relevant when assessing the appropriateness and legitimacy of political arrangements.

These differences are likely to have an important impact on political practice and theory. While there may be reasons to think that persons have a common rational "core" or essence, I argue that it is a dangerous mistake to think that this has many practical consequences for liberal politics. Persons in liberal democratic states may well be essentially rational individuals – but if they are, they are individuals who have been shaped (and continue to be shaped) in important ways by the veils with which they live.

The value of this non-essentialist or "operational" conception of persons is most obvious when we try to explain political behavior. Consider, for instance, the 2000 presidential debate at the University of Massachusetts at Boston. The candidates, then-Governor George W. Bush and Vice President Albert Gore, each appeared wearing a dark blue suit, red tie, white shirt, and black shoes. The stage was adorned with the Great American Seal, an elaborate symbol consisting of the image of a bald eagle clenching a scroll adorned with a motto, "The Union and the Constitution Forever," in its beak. The eagle holds an olive branch in its right talons and a cluster of arrows in its left, and is positioned on the triangular seal with an American flag.

This example is rich with veils. The Great Seal and the flags displayed prominently on stage are symbols that have been heavily invested with meaning and value over the years.[6] For that matter, nearly everything the candidates do in this forum – from wearing the unofficial "uniform" (indicating, presumably, an appropriate demeanor and seriousness) to greeting family members afterward – is ritualistic in nature and invested with some symbolic meaning.

What should we make of these rituals? One might easily take the quasi-official "uniform" of presidential candidates – as well as the totally predictable format, style of speech, and formalities – to be merely matters of convention. However, the persistent use of these veils suggests that they are something more than mere convention or habit. That is, the existence of these veils suggests that whatever the essential nature of the citizens may be, they are persons who are moved by their veils, and that these veils are used *because* they meet some deep human need and are very effective at motivating persons and shaping their actions.[7]

---

[6] In the case of the Great Seal, this investment was quite intentional. The symbols brought together to form the Great Seal are rooted in Western history and tradition, with most of the images in the design being appropriated from biblical and classical traditions. The committee appointed in July of 1776 to design the Great Seal consisted of Benjamin Franklin, Thomas Jefferson, and John Adams, a fact that suggests how seriously the framers took this task.

[7] As suggested in Chapter 1, there is a large group of practices that, in addition to their obvious practical uses, have important functions as political veils; once we understand the role of veils, we can see them all over the liberal democratic spectrum. Perhaps the clearest examples can be found in the use of monuments and official buildings as backdrops to protests and demonstrations. Surely the reasons and arguments underlying the civil rights movement and the pro-choice (or pro-life) positions are the same whether they are presented in an unadorned

This observation about persons is, again, practical, not metaphysical; it rejects not the essentialist account of persons, but the model of motivation suggested by that view of personhood.[8] By adopting the operational conception of personhood, we get a much richer way of representing the various factors that act on persons.

As indicated by the preceding example, this conception helps us to explain common political phenomena. It also has important implications for judgments about what our political arrangements *ought* to be. This is suggested by the fact that many recent race-, class-, and gender-focused approaches to political philosophy have rejected the more abstract, "thin" view of personhood in favor of a more full-blooded operational view. For instance, in his recent book *The Racial Contract*, Charles Mills objects that John Rawls's theory of justice is impoverished because it fails to take particular, historically contingent conditions (such as the lasting effects of slavery and racism) into consideration. While Mills does not regard these specific qualities as essential for personhood, he still maintains that they are relevant to political considerations in ways that are easily overlooked if we focus too closely on persons conceived in a completely abstract and general way.[9]

To be fair to Rawls, however, Mills's is a rather myopic snapshot of Rawls. A closer reading of Rawls tells us another story, a historically contingent story about Western liberal democracy in which the development of liberal democracy turns crucially on events that led first to a modus vivendi and then matured into the modern liberal value of

---

way or on the steps of the Supreme Court. The fact that they are more memorable when articulated in the second way tells us something about what really succeeds in motivating people.

Again, I do not deny that persons have a common – perhaps even essential – rational nature. My claim is simply that whatever our essential nature, persons are highly influenced by veils. That is the view of persons that is most relevant to policy makers, and, I believe, is one that deserves more attention in political theory.

[8] The conflict between this operational view of persons and the essentialist view is, in that sense, distinct from that between Rawls's neo-Kantian view of persons in *A Theory of Justice* (Cambridge, MA: Harvard University Press, 1971) and Michael J. Sandel's view given in *Liberalism and the Limits of Justice* (New York: Cambridge University Press, 1996). Theirs is a metaphysical debate about persons; mine is not.

[9] See also Susan Moller Okin, *Justice, Gender, and the Family* (New York: Basic Books, 1989), which illustrates the effects of enriching the range of qualities deemed relevant to judgments in moral or political philosophy (particularly qualities such as sex and ethnicity).

tolerance.[10] In other words, the contingent historical events in the West prepared people for liberal democracy:

We are not trying to find a conception of justice suitable for all societies regardless of their particular social or historical circumstances.... We look to ourselves and to our future, and reflect upon our disputes since, let's say, the declaration of independence. How far the conclusions we reach are of interest to a wider context is a separate issue....

.... What justifies a conception of justice is not its being true to an order antecedent to and given to us, but its congruence with our deeper understanding of ourselves and our aspirations, and our realization that, *given our history and the traditions embedded in our public life, it is the most reasonable doctrine for us.*[11]

In appealing to this tradition in his analysis of the conception of justice, Rawls acknowledges the importance of the operational view of persons. As a matter of philosophical principle, Rawls assumes that underlying this historically conditioned veneer is an abstract rational deliberator. Nonetheless, the stubborn effects of history are hard for even a philosopher to ignore.

2.2. LUCK AND LIBERALISM

The preceding quotation from Rawls suggests that even traditional liberal political philosophers recognize the important effect of non-essential characteristics of persons. By appealing to the historically contingent character of citizens of Western liberal polities, theorists can give a quite detailed (and compelling) account of the nature and justification of Western liberal institutions.

At the same time, this quotation also indicates an important limitation of Rawls's work – a limitation that becomes quite significant if we are interested in extending the range of liberal political institutions. That is, since the analyses offered by liberal theorists such as Rawls depend on a particular historical context, they will have little to say about the prospects of liberal democracy where those circumstances don't obtain. This is not to deny the importance of Rawls's insights and analysis, but

[10] This historical narrative is much clearer in "The Idea of an Overlapping Consensus," *Oxford Journal of Legal Studies* 7 (1987), pp. 1–25, and *Political Liberalism* (New York: Columbia University Press, 1993) than in Rawls's earlier work.
[11] John Rawls, "Kantian Constructivism in Moral Theory," *Journal of Philosophy* 77 (Summer 1980), pp. 518–19, emphasis added.

only to point out that they apply to a very specific situation: that of the West that gave birth to liberal democracy. The price of focusing on these particular societies is the risk of irrelevance of the resulting theory for those who have very different histories from people in the West, yet still desire liberal democracy.[12]

Between non-liberal states and well-entrenched, stable liberal states is a chasm unbridged by contemporary liberal theorists, and as far as one can tell from existing accounts, chance or good fortune seems to be the only way across this divide. Those in the West might congratulate themselves on their good fortune in this respect, but where does this leave the rest of the world? That is, where does that leave many nations in Africa, the Middle East, South America, and Asia that are anxious to democratize?

It is not surprising that liberal theorists (largely Westerners themselves) should overlook the special problems associated with extending the bounds of liberalism. In part, this is part of a general neglect of the developing world. More significantly, it reflects a common assumption that there is little one can do to create the conditions required for a liberal democracy except to wait for a lucky break. John Stuart Mill, for instance, claimed that "A nation ... cannot choose its form of government. The mere details, and practical organization, it may choose; but the essence for the whole, the seat of the supreme power, is determined for it by social circumstances."[13] He continued by claiming that:

Liberty, as a principle, has no application to any state of things anterior to the time when *mankind have become capable of being improved by free and equal discussion.* Until then, there is nothing for them but implicit obedience to an Akbar or a Charlemagne *if they are so fortunate as to find one.*[14]

Mill's is a rather pessimistic view that leaves the conditions for liberty largely to chance. Veil politics is intended to counteract this pessimism by supplying the tools for building the foundation of liberal democracy

---

[12] In citing the preceding quotation from Rawls in "Minority Culture and Cosmopolitan Alternative" (*University of Michigan Journal of Law Reform* 25, September 1992, p. 774), Jeremy Waldron notes this, and is clearly disturbed that Rawls's views on liberalism appear to be a local affair suitable only for Rawls's own culture.

[13] John Stuart Mill, *Utilitarianism, On Liberty, Considerations on Representative Government, Remarks on Bentham's Philosophy,* ed. Geraint Williams (London: J. M. Dent, 1993), p. 196.

[14] Ibid., p. 79 (emphasis added).

without simply having to assume that the contingent events that laid the foundations for current liberal democracies will exist elsewhere. As such, it provides the means for bridging this chasm between non-liberal states and well-entrenched, stable liberal institutions, and suggests that we can establish and maintain liberal democracy by appealing to customs, history, and traditions, rather than relying solely on chance to deliver it into our laps.

In putting forth veils as a means of transforming non-liberal states into stable, thriving liberal states, I do not mean to suggest that veil politics is a panacea, nor do I mean to imply that reason is irrelevant in this process. My claim is only that reason's role in politics is limited, and that veils can serve as tools for doing what reason cannot do. Part of the "balancing act" required for a liberal who wants to make use of veils is to show that reason and veils can work together for liberal democratic purposes. To understand the complexities involved in this balance, however, we need to turn our attention to the special role that rationality plays in liberal political theory, and see how the use of veils complements this role.

2.3. LIBERAL DEMOCRATIC THEORY AND RATIONALITY

To see why veil politics is needed to complement the role of rationality in liberal democracies, it is useful to take a closer look at the view that liberal democratic philosophers have traditionally held about reason and its relationship to political arrangements. The salient feature of this relationship is that liberals typically insist that reason should be in control of political matters. Harboring deep (and quite legitimate) suspicions about non-rational forces and their potential abuse, liberal theorists look to reason as a way of reining in those forces. While they may be an inevitable part of human life, these non-rational forces must be governed by reason in order for us to institute and maintain fair and equitable political arrangements.

A natural place to look for the origins of this view is in the political thought of Plato who, in *The Republic*, divided the soul into three parts and charged reason with the responsibility of regulating and harmonizing the passions. In the political realm he proceeded in a similar way, dividing society into three social classes and giving the philosopher (who, presumably, is the embodiment of reason) control over the others.

As Stuart Hampshire observes, this hierarchical view of the soul has worked its way deep into Western conceptions of the self – but not necessarily all for the good:

Unfortunately this fairy tale about parts of the soul and their hierarchy passes into common speech and into the vocabulary of the Latin language and hence into much of Christian philosophy. The corollary in ordinary and conventional speech has been that the desires and emotions of persons are supposed to issue from the quarrelsome and insubordinate underclass in the soul and that they should be left in their proper place and kept away from the serious business of self control.[15]

Privileging reason marginalizes the role of non-rational forces – desires, emotions, ambitions, and what Plato called *thymos*.[16] When reason is accorded this privilege, the passions and other non-rational aspects of human life become just so much noise that must be ignored or filtered out before one can get to the serious study of politics. Reason, as Carl Schmitt suggests, has been transformed by political theorists into a form of "mathematical ethics" that has:

[replaced] the concrete person of the king with an impersonal *authority* and a universal *reason*. The king must obey the law as the body obeys the soul. The universal criterion of the law is deduced from the fact that law (in contrast to will or the command of the concrete person) is only *reason*, not desire, and that it has no passions, whereas "a concrete person is moved by a variety of *passions*."[17]

Charles Frankel has made a similar point, observing that liberals "cherished the dream that, by some act of philosophic and semantic surgery, the power of symbols can be cut off and the irrational spurs to action expelled from organized life."[18]

---

[15] Stuart Hampshire, "Liberalism: The New Twist," *New York Review of Books* 40 (August 12, 1993), pp. 44–6.

[16] *Thymos* is a concept tied to the idea of self-esteem or self-respect, what Hegel refers to as the desire for recognition. This concept, according to Francis Fukuyama, is prevalent in the history of social and political philosophy: "Plato spoke of *thymos*, or 'spiritedness,' Machiavelli of man's 'desire for glory,' Hobbes of his pride or vainglory, Rousseau of his amour proper, Alexander Hamilton of the love of fame and James Madison of ambition, Hegel of recognition, and Nietzsche of man as the 'beast with red cheeks' " (*The End of History and the Last Man*, New York: Avon Books, 1992, p. 162).

[17] Carl Schmitt, *The Crisis Of Parliamentary Democracy*, transl. by Ellen Kennedy (Cambridge, MA: MIT Press, 1994), p. 42.

[18] Charles Frankel, "Political Symbols," *Antioch Review* 13 (Summer 1953), p. 353.

This preoccupation with reason and rationality has had striking implications for how political philosophers conceive of political and social life. In studying any phenomenon, we discriminate between those features deemed relevant to the phenomenon and those considered irrelevant to it. For instance, to explain why a dropped ball falls the way it does, only a few characteristics – its mass and its distance from the Earth – are considered relevant; the rest of its many properties are ignored. In precisely the same way, analysis of political institutions involves discriminating between relevant and irrelevant differences. The liberal conceit is that we can ignore non-rational factors without losing anything important to our understanding of politics.

But it is far from clear that we can either dispense with these non-rational factors or control them with reason. Love of country, for instance, can be a powerful source of civic virtue, yet as David Weberman explains, love for an object – be it a person or a country – is not obviously a matter of rational deliberation:

It should be obvious to all but the most mercenary that love is not an emotion that simply follows from the discovery of a sufficient number or kind of qualities possessed by the beloved. It seems patently false to think that love results from a series of judgments about the beloved. Rather there is every reason to think that it is the other way around. Love and other strong interpersonal attachments such as friendship, whatever their mysterious origins may be, are such that once they are in place, they reveal the beloved as having features (such as lovableness) apparent to the lover (perhaps *only* to the lover).... The same goes for mirth or amusement. We find ourselves amused by a story and in so doing discover it to be funny. This seems much more plausible than to think that we first acquire the belief that the story is funny and then as if by inference, "emote" or feel mirth or amusement.[19]

Tradition, rituals, symbols – all these operate on us in ways that circumvent obvious rational deliberation. And because of this element of

[19] David Weberman, "Heidegger and the Disclosive Character of Emotions," *Southern Journal of Philosophy* 3 (1996), p. 392. Weberman's point can also be seen in the case of a friend of mine who wears a T-shirt and baseball hat emblazoned with the title "The Greatest Dad on Earth." His children gave it to him on Fathers' Day and almost certainly believe what it says, despite having done little research comparing him to other fathers. Here, just as in Weberman's example of loving, the attitude appears to be prior to any operation of reason or reflection.

non-rationality, orthodox liberal theorists tend to conceive of tradition as antithetical to freedom of individuals' reason and self-determination.[20]

This general suspicion of non-rationality is, to be fair, not without justification, and liberal democracy today may largely be a reaction to the excesses of what I have called opaque pre-Enlightenment political arrangements. That is, while citizens played a role in the political structure, they lacked an effective voice in their own governing and were largely left in the dark as to the actual sources of political authority. But while mythic narratives may have been effective ways of motivating citizens, they were also easily abused.

This arrangement had a clear conservative bent, since the political order was presumably the creation of long-gone agents who could no longer be contacted for amendments to the original appointments. In that sense, the governed were heteronomous agents, ones robbed of self-determination by the ruling myths. And since the foundation of the political system denied even the possibility of amending the system, the prospects of changing the status quo from within the system were dim.

In the face of opaque political arrangements such as these, it is not surprising that some would react by stressing the importance of the autonomy of individuals, and by insisting that political power be legitimized by the rational consent of autonomous individuals. The long-term effect of this was the transformation of politics into a purely human affair modeled on contractual agreements among individuals. As such, the core of liberalism became individualism, and political theory turned to focus on freedom to determine one's destiny according to one's conscience and, more particularly, one's own reason.

Adopting this conception of a person as an essentially rational agent has important implications for liberal political theory, and even a cursory review of the literature shows that the concept of rationality has come to play a key role in liberal political philosophy. Rawls, for instance, asserts that "Any workable political conception ... must endorse rationality as a basic principle of political and social organization,"[21] while Jean Hampton claims, "Reason is the tool by which liberal states govern."[22]

---

[20] See Hans-Georg Gadamer, *Truth and Methods* (New York: Continuum, 1994), pp. 277–85.

[21] Rawls, *Political Liberalism*, p. 177. For a comprehensive catalogue of Rawls's use of "reasonable" and cognate terms, see Leif Wener, "Political Liberalism: An Internal Critique," *Ethics* 106, No. 1 (October 1995), p. 34.

[22] Jean Hampton, "The Common Faith of Liberalism," *Philosophical Quarterly*, 75 (1994), p. 193.

When we look at persons only in terms of their rational capacities, it is natural to think of their political arrangements as the result of only rational deliberation and negotiation – that is, as a *social contract*, a (hypothetical) deal cut among rational agents for the purpose of securing their own interests. The conceptual device of the social contract is particularly useful for liberal purposes by virtue of its transparency. Individuals *choose* to enter contracts and sign the contract for *themselves*, not on behalf of their family members, lineage, ethnic groups, religions, or races.

The identification, formulation, and justification of fundamental social and political principles has been the goal of virtually all social contract theorists since Locke. In this tradition, a state is legitimate only if each party has some appropriate *internal* reason to adopt and support society's overarching political and social principles. In this way, fundamental political values are decided upon by the operation of human reason. To the question "Why obey the law?" or "Why be loyal to the state?" the citizen of a liberal regime should be able to respond, "Because I have consented to do these things."

As used by Locke, Hobbes, and Rousseau, the social contract arises from an original "state of nature" where individuals are assumed to live without governmental constraints. From this condition, individuals come together and consent to a state structured in a way to guarantee their safety, freedom, or property against either external forces or each other. The binding nature of the agreement they make is that the parties each consented to it.

For contemporary philosophers such as John Rawls just as much as for these earlier thinkers, the consent of rational agents is the source of legitimacy of political institutions:

Our exercise of political power is proper and hence justifiable only when it is exercised in accordance with the constitution the essentials of which all citizens may reasonably be expected to endorse in light of principles and ideals acceptable to them as reasonable and rational. This is the liberal principle of legitimacy. To this it adds that all questions arising in the legislature that concern or border on constitutional essentials, or basic questions of justice, should also be settled, so far as possible, by principles and ideals that can be similarly endorsed. Only a political conception of justice that all citizens might be reasonably expected to endorse can serve as a basis of public reason and justification.[23]

---

[23] Rawls, *Political Liberalism*, p. 137.

The appeal of this approach is obvious. If, after all, the principles of a political system are ones to which all rational individuals have consented or would consent, what could be grounds for *rejecting* those principles? But it is one thing to see the appeal of an object, and quite another to show that we can obtain that object. And, I will argue, there are serious obstacles standing in the way of realizing this reason-based liberal system.

2.3.1. On the Problem of Pluralism

For justifying political principles, the model of a contract among rational, well-informed agents is quite compelling. But justification is only one of the problems we face in formulating political principles; the other is to ensure that those principles produce a stable society, one in which citizens are motivated to act in the ways they have agreed to act. Can this thin conception of persons as rational, self-interested agents provide the motivation needed to establish and maintain core liberal democratic values?

One reason to think it cannot do this by itself stems from the diversity of liberal states. The value of diversity in such states is seldom questioned, and tolerance of varying and incompatible conceptions of the good is a hallmark of modern liberalism.[24] But the diversity rightly cherished by liberals is not without limits. Fundamental political values such as peace, stability, liberty, loyalty to the state, and respect for the law tie disparate individuals and groups together; significant diversity with respect to *these* values undermines a state instead of strengthening it.

One often finds advocates of liberal democracy mounting passionate defenses of diversity – often enough, in fact, to suspect that the unity required for the thriving liberal state that makes liberty possible has come to be taken for granted. Judith Shklar suggests that one reason for this lack of concern for the grounds of social unity and cohesion is that the West, and particularly the United States, has enjoyed an unusually

---

[24] With respect to tolerance, liberalism comes in different forms, from those that give pride of place to autonomy (perhaps at the expense of many ways of life) to a "reformation" variant that emphasizes diversity and a commitment to protecting a wide range of lifestyles. For details concerning the two strands of liberalism, see William Galston, "Two Concepts of Liberalism," *Ethics* 105 (April 1995), pp. 516–34.

long and uninterrupted period of freedom and order, with the consequence that its people have experienced and remember mostly peaceful times. This, however, makes theorists who have known nothing but this remarkable stability particularly ill equipped to deal with significant degrees of diversity.

Yet growing diversity is likely to be one of the great challenges liberalism faces in the future. Historically, liberalism has had a basic commitment to allowing for significant variations in the religious, ethical, philosophical, and metaphysical ideals of life their members may pursue. In many ways, of course, diversity is welcome, enhancing as it does both the quality of citizens' lives and their freedom to pursue the kind of life they desire. Allowed the freedom to live their lives in a wide variety of ways, individuals can navigate life in an interesting and rewarding way, adopting conceptions of the good life as they see fit, and revising or dropping them as they see fit.

But there is a less attractive side to diversity. The people one sees in de facto liberal democratic states are seldom as one-dimensional as they are represented in theory. They may in the abstract be assumed to be equally rational and equally capable of dropping old ways and adopting new ones as they please, but their actual lives tell a different, substantially more complex story. Many people are respectful of others, but it is clear that many others are not – and may even take pleasure in disrespecting others. Many are committed to tolerance, while others cannot stand the fact that their children will have to share classrooms and playgrounds with children of other races and ethnicities. These are uncomfortable facts of liberal democratic states.

The fact of pluralism, then, poses a deep problem for liberal states. Jeremy Waldron captures the potential for conflict among individuals and groups who are united by a commitment to liberty:

People in fact exhibit different basic wants and needs, different fundamental beliefs about the world, and utterly disparate modes of reasoning. More seriously, it is arguable that many individual and communal commitments do not have the shape that the liberal envisages. Some people's commitments are so overwhelming that they appear to swamp the basic human concerns.... Other people's commitments are so inexplicably bound up with the sense of themselves that they find it impossible to abstract from them: they will be repelled by the thought that their ideals share a common form with those of people they despise, and they will be outraged that political justification should require them to think that way. Even more worryingly, some may find themselves with commitments so fervent that they cannot be pursued *except through the endeavor to impose them on others*.[25]

Here, Waldron speaks directly to the challenge to the signature liberal value of tolerance. Against the background of the thin conception of persons, the traditional liberal argument for toleration may go something like this: Reasonable people can disagree about conceptions of the good and other philosophical and moral issues. The results of good reasoning are plural, because people can reason correctly but reach different good conclusions. As a consequence, society should be tolerant of different views among its citizens. William Galston makes a similar argument, claiming that reasonable people can conflict, since political judgments cannot be reduced to a single measure, and one cannot give a single heterogeneous value absolute priority over all the others. "The most difficult choices in politics," Galston concludes, "are not between good and evil but between good and good."[26]

It is against the pluralism of de facto liberal states that orthodox liberalism's thin conception of rational persons must be assessed. That is, we must consider how effectively appeals to rationality *alone* can secure specific liberal values (for example, liberty, equality, justice, respect for laws, toleration, and participation), as well as more general values (such as peace, stability, loyalty, and political cohesion).[27] The peculiar aspect of liberal democratic political arrangements is that there is room for opposition, for protest, and for social critics, and this must be worked into the constitution of the political order. The question is how to balance these two demanding constitutional courses of action. I will argue that reason alone cannot hold the center. We must consider veil politics.

2.3.2. *On the Limits of Rationality*

Two excesses: to exclude reason, to admit nothing but reason.

Pascal, *Pensés*[28]

---

[25] Jeremy Waldron, "Theoretical Foundations of Liberalism," reprinted in *Liberal Rights: Collected Papers 1981–1991* (New York: Cambridge University Press, 1993), p. 57.

[26] William A. Galston, "Value Pluralism and Political Liberalism," *Philosophy and Public Policy* 16 (Spring 1996), p. 10.

[27] See William Galston, *Liberal Purposes* (New York: Cambridge University Press, 1991), especially Part III, for a detailed discussion of political values at large and liberal democratic ones in particular.

[28] Blaise Pascal, *Pensées*, trans. A. J. Krailsheimer (Penguin: London, 1966), p. 85.

As suggested previously, rationality has both *explanatory* and *justificatory* roles in liberal political philosophy. To see the extent to which rationality actually can satisfy each of these role, however, we need to fill in some of the details of the nature of rationality. Unfortunately, political philosophers have not often been clear when specifying what rationality is. Because of that, I present a definition of rationality that, while perhaps differing from what some liberal theorists have in mind, is one that will help to make the issues tractable.

For present purposes, I will focus on two traditional and widely used notions of rationality, which I will refer to as "absolute" and "instrumental."[29] "Absolute" versions characterize rationality in terms of a method for drawing inferences and assessing evidence; typically, this understanding of rationality places a premium on logical consistency, the use of deductive logic, and the presentation of evidence and reasons.

"Instrumental" views, on the other hand, characterize rationality in terms of how well an agent's chosen means help her to achieve particular ends. On this view, an agent is rational if, among all her considered beliefs or options, she adopts the most efficient means to her end – whatever that end might be. This type of rationality is often associated with the rational economic agent who acts in order to maximize her expected utility.

No matter which way rationality is characterized, it is supposed to establish, support, and legitimize liberal political arrangements and processes. As I shall argue, however, neither of these two characterizations of rationality can do all of these things. "Absolute" conceptions of rationality are ideally suited for characterizing the kind of deliberative process associated with liberalism. If, that is, rationality is a matter of deliberating in a particular way, then liberal values can be built into this procedure. One might think of rationality, for instance, as implying some kind of empathy for others, a recognition that others have aims different from your own. If this is a component of rationality, then this baseline level of "rational empathy" would help us to argue that a rational agent actually would choose liberal political principles.

---

[29] This is *not* presented as an exhaustive analysis of rationality. Any complete analysis should discuss alternative conceptions of rationality, but for present purposes, we can ignore these details.

Unfortunately, such an account lacks motivational force, in the sense that it cannot answer the question, Why be rational? What this conception fails to provide is a connection between being rational and a motivation for the agent doing what rationality dictates. It may justify, but it does not motivate.

"Instrumental" conceptions, on the other hand, *do* provide a practical reason to be rational, since they maintain that to be rational requires acting in a ways that help to get you what you want. They thus provide both a justification for acting in a particular way and a motivation for being rational. The problem with these conceptions, however, is that they leave the "ends" or "aims" of the rational agent up for grabs. Indeed, the reason such conceptions can account for the intuitive value of rationality is just because rationality is an all-purpose tool, one whose value is independent of the agent's aims. This means that this conception, too, is of limited use for the liberal, since the fact that it doesn't fix the aims of rational agents means it cannot give us a clear reason to think that rational agents must pursue liberal aims.

The fundamental problem with the orthodox liberal order is that the distance between the liberal democratic representation of persons and their de facto nature is so great. The thin view of the rational person is but a pale shadow of real people, the people you find in the factory trying to make a living, in the aggressive business world trying to make money, in the farm, at worship in the church, at home trying to get the children to carry on the family values. The abstract liberal representation may correctly identify the common rational core of all these individuals, but appealing to *just* this core is bound to be in vain. The gulf between the rational person and the full-blooded citizen is so wide that any attempt to get people to reason the way that traditional liberals prescribe is bound to be repressive, oppressive, paternalistic, and brutally coercive and in violation of the liberal principle order of self-determination.

This kind of appeal isn't doomed to failure as long as conditions are right. The problem is that relying on circumstances being right amounts to counting on good fortune. When fortune is *not* with us, the liberal is left with either writing off the people who aren't "prepared" in the right way or coercing them.

It follows from this that with respect to political values that a liberal state wants to establish legitimately, there is no guarantee that instrumental rationality will lead us to support the liberal order. It can lead us *against* it. This implication is clearly brought out in David Hume's insistence that:

'Tis not contrary to reason to prefer the destruction of the whole world to the scratching of my finger. 'Tis not contrary to reason for me to [choose] my total ruin, to prevent the least uneasiness of an *Indian* or person wholly unknown to me. 'Tis as little contrary to reason to prefer even my own acknowledg'd lesser good to my greater, and have a more ardent affection for the former than the latter.[30]

If one thinks of rationality in instrumental terms, then it is easy to see that ultimate ends – that objective for which all actions are ultimately taken – cannot be justified in any (instrumentally) rational manner: If those ends *were* rational, they would have to have instrumental value with respect to yet *another* end, which contradicts the assumption that those were ultimate ends in the first place. On the instrumental view of rationality, then, ultimate ends are not rationally discursive.

The rationalist now faces a dilemma, for no matter which conception of rationality she chooses, it is clear that rationality is not "self-supporting." Conceived of in the "instrumental" sense, reason requires an exogenous source of purpose or direction that itself is not determined by reason. Thought of in the "absolute" sense, reason requires a separate source of motivation. Under this "absolute" conception, then, there may be a variety of incompatible, but equally attractive, characterizations of rationality, none of which is capable of motivating individuals.

This suggests that reason alone will be incapable of supporting and sustaining the political and social values needed for a stable state, leaving the liberal with three options:

• Exclude individuals who happen to hold doctrines that are incompatible with liberal political arrangements.
• Leave it up to luck and hope that everything will work out.
• Use force to *compel* those individual to be rational.

When push comes to shove, these unpleasant alternatives force even those most dedicated to the use of reason in political arrangements into rather unattractive positions. Rousseau, for instance, had no recourse but to force when reason failed, claiming that people who could not

---

[30] David Hume, *A Treatise of Human Nature*, ed. L. A. Selby-Bigge (Oxford, UK: Clarendon Press, 1978), p. 416.

rationally discern that behaving according to the laws prescribed by the "common will" is in their self-interest should "be force to be free," and that in extreme cases of such irrationality, the person should be put to death.[31] Locke was led to a similarly unpleasant conclusion when he recommended that if a soldier cannot see that it is in his self-interest to defend the state, he should be hanged.[32]

On the same note, K. Anthony Appiah discusses the irrationality of racism and insists, "We do not need the full apparatus of Kantian ethics to require that morality be constrained by reason." But now look where his rationalism leads him: "Still, as I say, I do not know how I would argue against someone who could not see this; someone who continued to act on the contrary belief might, in the end, simply have to be locked up."[33]

2.4. CONCLUSION

The preceding discussion shows that rational politics must fit into a broader context that complements – but does not eliminate – the role of rational deliberation. This conclusion forces us to examine how fundamental political values are acquired, supported, and transmitted from one generation to the next, or in other words, how the state is reproduced. If political ends are simply left to chance, then there is little for us to do but hope that conditions are favorable, and prepare to use force to counteract the more dangerous threats.

---

[31] Jean-Jacques Rousseau, *The Basic Political Writings*, transl. by Donald A. Cress (Indianapolis, IN: Hackett, 1982), p. 226.
[32] As Strauss and Cropsey (*History of Political Philosophy*, Chicago, IL: University of Chicago Press, 3rd edition, 1987, p. 509) point out, this hardly explains how a soldier who fails to embrace Locke's position will be motivated to sacrifice his own life for the sake of this end.
[33] The full citation reads thus:

A proper analogy would be with someone who thought that we could continue to kill cattle for beef, even if cattle exercised all the complex cultural skills of human beings. I think it is obvious that creatures like that share our capacity for understanding as well as our capacity for pain should not be treated the way we actually treat cattle; that "intrinsic speciesism" would be as wrong as racism. And the fact that most people think it worse to be cruel to dolphins suggests that they may agree with me. The distinction in attitudes surely reflects a belief in the greater richness of the mental life of large mammals. Still, as I say, I do not know how I would argue against someone who could not see this; someone who continued to act on the contrary belief might, in the end, simply have to be locked up (Kwame Anthony Appiah, *In My Father's House*, New York: Oxford University Press, 1992, p. 19).

I believe there is a third way, an option beyond passively waiting for circumstances to become favorable, but short of exercising force. Veil politics is a way to meet this extrarational need in liberal democracies. This question puts veil politics and its views on civic pedagogy, political rituals, symbol, tradition, myths, and rhetoric at center stage and, if I am right, compels even defenders of rationalistic politics to deal with them. Veil politics, then, brings good news for friends of liberal democracy, opening up as it does a new path to the establishment and maintenance of liberal states.

Chapter 3

Liberalism and Veil Politics

In the previous chapters, I have argued that we must clearly separate the task of *justifying* liberal political principles from that of *motivating* persons to act in accordance with them. Recognizing this difference helps us to avoid thinking that the mere fact that those principles are justified will assure that citizens will be motivated to act in accordance with them.

In particular, I have argued that we cannot rely on individuals to be moved to act as good liberals merely through the exercise of their rational faculties. Conceived of instrumentally, reason is represented as attaching to the "engine" of desire, directing and channeling the passions in an efficient – but not necessarily liberal – direction. Thought of in an absolute sense, rationality can be defined in a way that links it to liberal values. Doing this, however, effectively cuts off rationality from an individual's desires; the rational individual will be liberal, but there is no special motivation for anyone to be rational.

In claiming this, I do not intend to deny reason its essential role in liberalism, but rather to underscore one basic point: *For reason to lead to actions that are consistent with liberal principles, it must operate in the right kind of context of values.* The central challenge facing those who want to develop and sustain liberal institutions, then, is not simply to develop what we might call the "rational faculties" of individuals – the ability to weigh reasons and evidence and think abstractly – but also to create and maintain the aims and values appropriate for liberalism.

As a matter of history, the circumstances most appropriate for the development and flourishing of liberalism have been rare, limited mostly to Europe and North America. This shouldn't, of course, be taken as a sign of some special virtue of the West worthy of self-congratulation. If anything, the problem of entrenching liberal institutions in the

47

developing world – the problem of "nation-building" – suggests that the existence of these conditions requires the convergence of just the right social, economic, religious, or perhaps even very long-term geographical factors.[1]

The claim that there are preconditions for liberal institutions is un-controversial. Rawls, for instance, readily acknowledges the need for a modus vivendi (a kind of "Hobbesian peace") and minimal levels of welfare before any genuinely liberal state can exist. On Rawls's account, a crucial step in the path to this minimal level of tolerance was the wars of religion of the sixteenth and seventeenth centuries, which taught Europeans the hard way that they might be better off tolerating unwanted neighbors rather than living in continual war trying to eliminate them.

Acknowledging the long (and often bloody) evolution of liberal institutions is important for appreciating the nature of existing liberal democracies. More significantly, perhaps, is its importance when we consider the problems of spreading liberal democracy and sustaining it where it is only beginning to take root. That is, when we understand the complex history of present institutions, we are less likely to presume that those institutions will naturally take root when "transplanted" into societies that lack that history.

Many parts of the developing world, for instance, simply don't have the luxury of an existing modus vivendi, nor is it acceptable simply to hope that – by luck or historical accident – conditions will become favorable sometime in the future. Instead, we need to find some means of generating and nurturing these conditions in order to give liberalism a chance to take root.

Given the limits of rationality, we must look toward non-rational methods of shaping behavior and judgments – in other words, veils – and it is this that makes veil politics so important for both creating and sustaining liberal states. By drawing attention to the important role of customs, rituals, and symbols in defining the "terrain" on which individual rationality works, veil politics will help us to control those factors. The promise of veil politics is that it gives us a framework for thinking about how we can use features of the existing "symbolic terrain" that

---

[1] See, for instance, Jared Diamond's *Guns, Germs and Steel: The Fates of Human Societies* (New York: W. W. Norton, 1997), in which he claims that long-term factors such as geography, biodiversity, and climate, rather than short-term cultural factors, were most influential in leading to the political, economic, and military ascendancy of Europe over the rest of the world.

already influence behavior to alter that terrain in a way that makes it more amenable to liberal principles.

The claim that symbolic factors have a powerful effect on behavior is hardly controversial. *If* liberals can make the kind of deliberate, purposeful use of veils that I am advocating *without* violating their own principles, then they will have a powerful tool to put to work for liberal purposes. The main focus of this chapter is to show that the antecedent of this conditional holds, and that liberals can indeed use veils in a purposeful manner without compromising their fundamental values.

3.1. A CHALLENGE TO AUTONOMY?

The apparent tension between veil politics and liberalism is perhaps most obvious when we consider the value of autonomy. Before considering this tension, let us first consider some proposed characterizations of this concept. Autonomy has been variously defined and conceived as follows:

- "An autonomous agent must be independent-minded. He must not have to depend on others for being told what he is to think or do. . . . a person is autonomous to the degree that what he thinks and does cannot be explained without reference to his own activity of mind."[2]
- "An autonomous man . . . may do what another tells him, but not because he has been told to do it . . . . By accepting as final the command of others, he forfeits his autonomy . . . a promise to abide by the will of the majority creates an obligation, but it does so precisely by giving up one's autonomy."[3]
- "What is essential to the person's remaining autonomous is that in a given case his mere recognition that a certain action is required by law does not settle the question of whether he will do it."[4]
- Citizens "finally pass to the level of autonomy when they appreciate that rules are alterable, that they [rules] can be criticized."[5]

---

[2] R. S. Downe and Elizabeth Telfer, "Autonomy," *Philosophy* 46 (1971), p. 301.
[3] Robert Paul Wolff, *In Defense of Anarchism* (New York: Harper & Row, 1970), pp. 14, 41.
[4] Thomas Scanlon, "A Theory of Freedom of Expression," *Philosophy and Public Affairs* 1 (1972), p. 215.
[5] R. S. Peters, "Freedom and Development of the Free Man," in *Education and the Development of Reason*, ed. R. F. Dearden (London: Routlege and Kegan Paul, 1972), p. 130.

What these accounts suggest is that autonomy is a matter of keeping a critical distance from rules and institutions, a separation that allows the autonomous agent to see those rules and institutions as alterable through a process of self-conscious, rational deliberation.

This way of thinking about autonomy dovetails nicely with the sense of autonomy that lies at the heart of both Kant's and Mill's political philosophies. On these accounts, autonomy is conceived of in terms of self-determination, where reason is assumed to play the role of the "internal governor." In an explicitly political context, autonomy amounts to the ability of individuals to pursue their conceptions of the good free of external constraints; the autonomous agent is one who chooses *for herself* how her life goes rather than having it determined for her.

Conceived of in this way, the threat that the deliberate use of veils poses to autonomy seems quite clear, for opening the door to direct appeals to emotions and deeply entrenched traditions either circumvents a person's internal governor or drowns out the dictates of reason. Either way, it looks as if the individual is being controlled by the veils – and by extension, by the designer and manipulator of the veils.

One of the ways to see how the use of veils may threaten autonomy is to think in terms of access to information used in deliberations. Mill, for instance, clearly had in mind the role of deliberation in self-determination when he wrote that "He who lets the world or his own portion of it choose his plan of life for him has no need for any other faculty than the ape-like one of imitation."[6] To behave in an unreflective or imitative way is to surrender one's autonomy – to become heteronomous.

But if "ape-like imitation" characterizes the heteronomous individual, what are the salient features of the autonomous agent? Mill, at least, offers the following profile:

He who chooses his plan of life for himself employs all his faculties. He must use observation to see, reasoning and judgment to foresee, activity to gather materials for decision, discrimination to decide, and when he has decided, firmness and self-control to hold to his deliberate decision.[7]

According to Mill, then, being autonomous depends on three factors: one must have (i) *sufficient resolution* to carry through on decisions reached by

---

[6] Mill, *Utilitarianism, On Liberty, Considerations on Representative Government, Remarks on Bentham's Philosophy*, p. 126.
[7] Ibid.

(ii) *responsible deliberation* on the (iii) *relevant evidence*. It seems plausible to think this third condition requires having open access to information relevant for intelligent judgments. But in that case, veils will pose a problem, since by their very nature they obscure or hide information. Veils stand between an individual and truth, and so generally distort the truth in various ways, possibly – but not necessarily – misleading persons by sins either of omission or of commission. Transparency politics, on the other hand, directs us to maximize openness, and so would seem to be a natural fit with Mill and his view of autonomy.

For a utilitarian like Mill, the ultimate reason to support individual autonomy must rest on its propensity to increase overall happiness (or, more generally, overall utility). One's status as a moral agent depends on one's having utilities to maximize, or being capable of happiness and suffering; being autonomous is a general condition that seems a plausible tactic for maximizing the total utility in the population. If veils undermine autonomy, they should therefore be rejected (at least as a matter of principle) as being counterproductive from a utilitarian point of view.

Deontological theorists such as Kant make a similar appeal to the value of self-governance, but for fundamentally different reasons. From the Kantian perspective, autonomy has inherent value. Rather than being a means to the end of maximizing overall utility, autonomy – an individual's ability rationally to formulate laws and to impose those laws upon oneself – is what grants a person moral worth and dignity in the first place. As Kant claims:

What is it then that entitles a morally good attitude of mind, or virtue to make claims so high? It is nothing less than the *share* which it affords to a rational being in the making of universal law, and which therefore fits him to be a member in the possible kingdom of ends. . . . [T]he law-making which determines all value must for this reason have a dignity, that is, an unconditioned and incomparable worth, for the appreciation of which, as necessarily given by the rational being, the word "reverence" is the only becoming expression. *Autonomy* is therefore the ground of the dignity of human expression and of every rational nature.[8]

It is, of course, the intrinsic value of autonomous agents that underwrites Kant's famous dictum that we are morally obligated to treat such individuals always as ends in themselves, never as means.

---

[8] Immanuel Kant, *Groundwork of the Metaphysics of Morals*, trans. H. J. Paton (New York: Harper & Row, 1958), p. 103, emphasis added.

According to this tradition, moral agents act autonomously when their actions are determined by their reason, rather than by irrational impulses, habits, or emotions. On this view, a moral agent or a full-fledged citizen is essentially a rational deliberator, and it is only when her actions are determined by that rational nature that the citizen is genuinely self-governing. Other factors that might influence behavior – emotion, sentiment, habit, or tradition – are as distinct from the individual's rational nature as clothes are from the body, and a person is heteronomous to the degree that those "external" factors, rather than her own rational nature, determine her actions.

From Kant's perspective on autonomy, just as with Mill's, veil politics seems to pose an obvious problem. Here, however the problem doesn't lie in the effect of veils, but on the mere fact that veils are used in a deliberate, purposeful way to define and align individuals's ultimate political values. Given that veil politics stresses using them for this very intention, what could veil politics be if not a system for treating autonomous agents as means rather than ends?

3.2. VEILS AND LIBERAL PURPOSES

Veils, then, at least *appear* to conflict with two influential views of autonomy. Thus, it is not surprising that liberal theorists have traditionally viewed what I am calling veils – traditions, rituals, and emotionally laden symbols – with great suspicion. Indeed, there are good reasons to be concerned about possible abuses of veils. As I've noted previously, a person's demand to know the truth about political institutions typically arises not from idle curiosity, but from her desire to make intelligent choices that further her interests. Veils may misrepresent the truth about institutions, knowledge of which might often be quite relevant to individuals's judgments about those institutions. If others can control how those facts are represented (or misrepresented), the agent can be led to make decisions that she wouldn't have made had she been given the truth. In short, by allowing veils to stand between facts and citizens, we allow (and perhaps even condone) manipulation of those citizens, and given the risk of abuse of this kind, it might seem reasonable to insist on transparency politics.

On the face of it, then, it is hard to see how veils could fail in some way or another way to undermine autonomy, either by controlling the information available to citizens or by circumventing altogether the rational faculties of citizens. Hence, even veils that are used *by* liberals and *for* liberal purposes are problematic, and may be seen as a "selling out" of the liberal's fundamental commitment to individual autonomy.

Things, however, turn out to be more complicated than this. In particular, the notion of autonomy requires closer scrutiny, for the apparent conflict arises only given a simplified – and, I shall argue, unsustainable – view of autonomy. A closer look at the notion of autonomy (along with its complementary notion of coercion) will suggest how to reconcile liberalism with the methods of veil politics.

One point that is easy to overlook, but is also crucial for understanding how to reconcile liberalism with veil politics, is that autonomy cannot realistically be analyzed as an isolated concept, independent of all others. As I have noted previously, autonomy requires at least a "Hobbesian peace," a consensus that an uneasy truce with people you don't like is better than the alternative, a life of "continuell feare, and danger of violent death," one that is "solitary, poore, nasty, brutish and short."[9]

Without that minimal level of peace, individual autonomy simply cannot be actualized. Autonomy, then, is not and should not be treated as prior – logically or temporally – to all other political values, but can flourish only against a background of other preexisting values. Realizing the autonomy of individuals, then, requires that persons in some way form a consensus about the superiority of an uneasy peace to continual conflict; it is only *after* we secure this most fundamental kind of stability that we can begin to worry seriously about other values.

If we are interested is promoting autonomy, then, we should first consider how those prior conditions are established. As I have already noted, while modern liberal democratic theorists can point to historical events and factors that led to the stability underlying existing liberal states, they have remarkably little to say about how this basic level of peace could be achieved where is doesn't already exist.

On reflection, this silence shouldn't be particularly surprising. Modern democracies have, for the most part, enjoyed relatively long periods of internal peace; the most recent threats to Western democracies such as the United States and Great Britain have been external rather than the result of internal divisions. The relatively long history of internal consensus in such states has led many theorists to take it for granted. When we look beyond established democracies to the developing world, however,

---

[9] Thomas Hobbes, *Leviathan: of the Matter, Forme and Power of a Commonwealth Ecclesiasticall and Civil*, ed. Michael Oakshott (New York: Macmillan, 1962), p. 100.

it is apparent that we cannot simply assume that this basic level of peace and stability will obtain. Insofar as we are interested in spreading liberalism, this broad consensus is something we cannot simply assume and something we shouldn't simply leave to chance.

In this respect, I claim that veils have an important role in promoting autonomy by helping to support a cluster of values that support an underlying stability in the community. Veil politics creates the conditions that make individual autonomy possible. Liberal citizens enjoy their autonomy not in a vacuum but with a background of fundamental values such as peace, stability, and tolerance. The methods of veil politics give us ways both to create these conditions where they do not presently exist and to sustain them where they do. The challenge is to show how we can use the methods of veil politics without violating liberal principles.

3.3. TRADITION AND AUTONOMY

A natural way for liberals to think of the difference between autonomous and non-autonomous (or heteronomous) agents is in terms of the ability of a person to determine the course of her life by the use of her rational capacities. The self-governing person doesn't operate purely on instinct or habit, but by deliberating on the evidence and applying reason. Thus, in *On Liberty* Mill holds that "neither one person nor any number of persons is warranted in saying to another creature of ripe-years, what he shall do with his life, for his own, what he chooses to do."[10]

Self-control, in this sense, can be thought of as a matter of having one's actions determined by one's own reason rather than other "external" factors. It is this ability to determine one's own actions that is of paramount value for the liberal – even if individuals choose to lead lives that are not the best. For instance, one leading liberal theorist, Amy Gutmann, claims that:

Even if there were someone wiser than Socrates in our midst, she still could not claim the right to order the souls of all citizens. Just as an unexamined life is not

---

[10] Mill, *Utilitarianism, On Liberty, Considerations on Representative Government, Remarks on Bentham's Philosophy*, p. 144. Mill's reference to persons of "ripe-years" suggests that children should be regarded as potentially autonomous, and realize their potential by developing their rational faculties – a process that is typically a function of age and experience.

worth living, so too a good life must be one that a person recognizes as such, lived from the inside, according to one's own best lights.[11]

The issue, then, concerns the meaning of the locution "lived from the inside." In terms of veils, this question concerns the extent to which veils constitute an *external* factor that interferes with an agent's ability to govern herself. It might appear obvious that veils fall into this category, but a little reflection suggests that the issue is more complicated than it might seem. That is, the mere fact that veils are part of a person's external environment and affect her actions is no reason to think that manipulation of those veils robs her of autonomy; reasons and arguments have precisely this same status, but presumably are no threat to autonomy.

Discriminating between what we intuitively regard as the "right" kind of causes of autonomous action and the "wrong" ones thus requires a more subtle approach to autonomy and coercion. Mill himself gives us a promising way to draw these distinctions in his discussion of the relationship between culture and autonomy. He observes that:

A person whose desires and impulses are his own – are the expression of his own nature, *as it has been developed and modified by his own culture – is said to have a character.* One whose desires and impulses are not his own, has no character, no more than a steam-engine has character.[12]

On this view, autonomy requires not just the capacity for rational deliberation and reflection, but a kind of "ownership" of the elements of a culture or set of social and political institutions. The autonomous agent has a *character of her own*, a set of general dispositions, habits, intuitions, and values that, while 'bestowed' upon her by external circumstances, is her *own*. Her actions are rational, but spring from rationality operating on the values and aims that constitute her own full-blooded character. Far from undermining autonomy, cultural influences are regarded by Mill as helping to support autonomy by giving an agent "ownership" of particular desires.

Recognizing this relationship between autonomy and culture has two important consequences when we assess veil politics in terms of both its *effectiveness* in altering and maintaining political values and its

---

[11] Amy Gutmann, "Undemocratic Education," in *Liberalism and the Moral Life*, ed. Nancy Rosenblum (Cambridge, MA: Cambridge University Press, 1989), p. 72.

[12] Mill, *Utilitarianism, On Liberty, Considerations on Representative Government, Remarks on Bentham's Philosophy*, p. 128 (emphasis added).

justification at least in the minimal sense of being consistent with basic liberal principles.

3.3.1. *Autonomy through Tradition*

One of the problems with instilling and maintaining political values is that this is typically not amenable to conventional education; values are not learned like a rule or an equation.[13] This is a point that Mill, for one, clearly recognized:

[T]he capacity of any given people for fulfilling the conditions of any given form of government cannot be pronounced on by any sweeping rule. Knowledge of the particular people, and general practical judgement and sagacity, must be the guide.[14]

Effective political techniques are ones that take into account the nature of the people affected. Mill's own example was the way Italian patriots prepared the Italian people for "freedom in unity" by working within the existing tradition to create the demand for change. By acting in this evolutionary, rather than revolutionary, manner, they could tap into existing attachments to Italian culture, using them to support their changes.[15]

As a practical tool for political change, then, it makes sense to use *existing* resources – institutions, customs, and traditions – to generate support for *new* political arrangements:

When an institution, or a set of institutions, has the way prepared for it by the opinions, tastes, and habits of the people, they are not only more easily induced to accept it, but will more easily learn, and will be, from the beginning better disposed, to do what is required of them both for the preservation of the institutions, and for bringing them into such action as enables them to produce their best results. It would be a great mistake in any legislator not to shape his measures so as to take advantage of such *preexisting habits and feelings when available....* People are more easily induced to do, and to do more easily, what they are already used to; but people also learn to do things new to them. *Familiarity is a great help.*[16]

By focusing our attention on cultural factors, then, veil politics gives us a highly effective set of tools for controlling political values. If this

---

[13] See Chapter 5 for a more detailed discussion of the use of veils in civic education.
[14] Mill, *Utilitarianism, On Liberty, Considerations on Representative Government, Remarks on Bentham's Philosophy*, p. 194.
[15] Ibid., p. 195.
[16] Ibid. (emphasis added).

were incompatible with liberal values, of course, mere effectiveness would be of no use. However, thinking of autonomy in terms of acting within one's own culture also gives us a natural way to deal with the problem of the legitimacy of veils. That is, the difference between legitimate and illegitimate veils is essentially the difference in the way that a population's political values are changed.

This view may seem to be at odds with the traditional liberal theorist's view of an autonomous individual as an "unencumbered self," located outside of a tangle of history and tradition. However, once we move from the ethereal levels of theory to political practice, there are at least two compelling reasons to reject this rather abstract view of self-governance.

The first can be found in the origins of autonomous agents. Children provide the clearest example of this, since they start from a state in which (literal) paternalism is something we are obligated to impose to a state in which such control is oppressive. What makes the difference between these two states? At a very abstract level, the changes leading from the first state to the second could be described as the "development of her rational faculties". But closer inspection suggests that this maturation also includes a process of assimilation into a common culture and style of thought, one in which children internalize social and political norms much as they do natural language – that is, not by explicit education and training, but by immersion.

A second reason for rejecting the "unencumbered self" as the model of the autonomous person can be seen by looking at special cases of adults. For instance, it is commonly acknowledged that some adults – the mentally incompetent – suffer from deficiencies that rob them of their autonomy. More interesting are the cases of those who, while suffering no obvious cognitive problems, might also be seen as lacking the abilities required of citizens of liberal states – particularly those who have spent most of their adult lives in prison or who are recent immigrants.

It would be highly implausible to claim that persons in this category lack reason; all too often, turning to crime may be the most rational thing a person can do when placed in certain circumstances. Rather, what they lack is the ability to function in normal society in an appropriate way; they have not "internalized" the basic ideals of civil life. As such, examples like these suggest that becoming autonomous (in the sense relevant to liberalism) is not entirely a matter of cognitive ability, but also requires the development of particular social values. Further, if liberal theorists regard these groups of individuals as exceptional, they will essentially be washing their hands of the problem of transmitting political values – a problem that is particularly acute in states where immigration is significant.[17]

The intimate link between these internalized values and behavior indicates that any account of autonomy must accommodate the existence of tradition and custom. As Mill puts it, "it would be absurd to pretend that people ought to live as if nothing whatever had been known in the world before they came to it."[18] Mill's linking autonomy to operating within one's own culture, then, indicates that he sees autonomy not as requiring transcending tradition, but as exercising reason within the framework of values provided by one's own culture.[19]

While this appeal to tradition seems to fit poorly with the usual view of autonomy, it seems to capture many other quite strong intuitions. For instance, consider the colonization of Africa. In the clash of cultures, Europeans displaced existing political arrangements with arrangements and processes totally alien to the inhabitants. In so doing, Europeans left people without a character of their own, Mill's metaphorical "steam engines," governed by rules and dictates imposed from without. This seems to be a plausible example of how destroying the culture of a people can also undermine the autonomy of the colonized – even long after independence is gained.

Another way to see the important role that one's own culture plays in autonomy is to think in terms of what counts as coercion. To grow up in a culture naturally shapes the character of an individual – her aims, her values, and the methods she uses in making judgments – in ways of which she is quite unaware. But to call this process of enculturation "coercive" is to stretch the concept of coercion to the point of meaninglessness.

---

[17] The case of criminals in the United States is a particularly important and interesting one, given the large number of young adults – disproportionately African American males – incarcerated each year. Habits and practices developed in prison may often remain part of a person's character and can play an important role in determining how well a person fares after being freed. Even if liberals assume an existing liberal state with existing fundamental values, they still have to deal with these sorts of individuals, too numerous to be treated as ad hoc cases.

[18] Ibid., p. 125.

[19] For recent views on the important of culture to liberalism, see Will Kymlicka, *Liberalism, Community, and Culture* (Oxford, UK: Clarendon Press, 1989); Jeremy Waldron, "Multiculturalism and Melange," pp. 90–118, and Kwame Anthony Appiah, "Culture, Subculture, Multiculturalism," *Public Education in a Multicultural Society*, ed. Robert K. Fullinwider (New York: Cambridge University Press, 1996), pp. 65–89.

3.3.2. Tradition and Coercion

This does not, of course, mean that there is nothing that is properly re-garded as coerced action. For instance, there is an obvious difference between a physics teacher *asking* students to solve a set of physics prob-lems by Friday and *threatening* to lock them up unless they do so. In the latter case, it makes sense to say that the teacher is coercing an agent, but the former (asking students to solve a physics problem by Friday) does not seem to be a case of coercion at all.

Note, however, that the difference between the two is not that *external* forces play a role in the latter but not the former case – external forces are present in each case, either in the form of a request or of a threat. Rather, the essential difference seems to be the "path" that those external forces take in determining the student's action. External forces are common to both autonomous and coerced or heteronomous actions. To think that autonomy requires being free of *any* external interference is too restric-tive to be believable.

The key difference between legitimate and illegitimate liberal veils is that the former respect the existing culture, while the latter do not. Appeals to tradition can be thought of as non-coercive tools that, when used in the service of liberalism, can help to instill the values that make liberty and autonomy possible.[20]

We can see this process at work in Mill's account of the development of liberal states. For Mill, the existence of free societies is not simply a random event. It is ultimately guided by a common arbiter of mutually shared behavior or values, that is, the fundamental political values of the society or what Mill refers to as "freedom in unity." It is against the background of shared ultimate political and social values that in-dividuals in the liberal state that Mill advocates enjoy their right to autonomy.

If Mill's discussion of customs strikes liberal political theorists as contradicting his championing of autonomy and progress, it is because they fail to acknowledge that his conception of liberty involves a shared framework of political values that results from combining both the lib-eral and the pre-liberal tradition. This hybrid framework allows people

---

[20] I note that the cultural condition referred to here is a necessary, but not a sufficient condition for autonomy. That is, my claim that autonomy is ultimately contingent on culture does not commit me to claiming that, if one grows up in a highly illiberal culture then one is autonomous as long as one's submissive character is the product of one's culture.

to act rationally with respect to social and political ends that are appropriate for the liberal society that he advocates.

Rousseau also held views similar to Mill's about institution building. Despite his radical views on individuality, rationality, and freedom, when confronted with the question of institution building or with the establishment of the groundwork for democratic order, Rousseau himself calls on historical, social, and cultural factors to do the initial work of establishing peace and order:

> The wise men who want to speak to the common masses in the former's own language rather than in the common vernacular cannot be understood by the masses. For there are a thousand kinds of ideas that are impossible to translate in the language of the populace.... Since, therefore, the legislator is incapable of using either force or reasoning, he must of necessity have recourse to an authority of a different order, *which can compel without violence and persuade without convincing*.
>
> This is what has always forced the fathers of nations to have recourse to the intervention of heaven and to credit gods with their own wisdom ... in the formation of man and of the city [so that people] might obey with liberty and bear with docility the yoke of public felicity....
>
> We should not ... conclude from this that politics and religion have a common object among us, but that in the beginning stages of nations the one serves as an instrument of the other.[21]

Like Mill, Rousseau acknowledges that liberty can flourish only given some antecedent civil order, and that reason alone cannot be considered a reliable means of reaching that initial order. For liberals, the value of veils is that they give us a way of producing the conditions needed for liberty that is consistent with liberal values.

3.4. JUSTIFICATION FOR VEILS

In the preceding section, I have argued that there is no necessary conflict between the use of veils and liberalism; while there are surely many uses of veils that conflict with liberalism, this clash is due to particular features of those veils, not merely to their *being* veils. In that case, what sort of veils can one accept? In the abstract, liberals must reject those that are coercive or do not promote liberal values. But which are these? In order to make these more practical judgments, we need some way to

---

[21] Jean-Jacques Rousseau, *The Basic Political Writings*, trans. Donald A. Cress (Cambridge, UK: Hackett Publishing Company, 1978), pp. 164–5.

distinguish those veils that are compatible with liberalism from those that are not.

This discrimination can be done along two different axes: effectiveness and legitimacy. The first of these depends on how efficiently or reliably the veils achieve their intended purpose. The second is a matter of how well those veils serve specifically liberal purposes, and how consistent the operation of those veils is with liberal principles.

If we want effective veils, it is sensible to use ones that are already familiar to citizens. Veils must be fastened to customs latent in the contingent culture of the polity rather than from totally foreign material. Take the example of the myth or veil in the United States of young George Washington chopping down the cherry tree. This veil is not intended to plant false belief or instill some malign values into the citizenry (or future full members of the liberal state) but to instill the virtue of honesty. For a child, the idea of Washington admitting that he cut down the cherry tree could be exciting and civically uplifting in ways that can easily lead to political habit formation.

An ineffective veil would substitute for the cherry tree something less familiar – say, a baobab tree, which is native to West Africa. The problem with that is that American children will find it difficult to understand the references to a baobab tree, and so could render the veil moot. Similar problems can also arise when veils become too obtrusive, for example, when we become aware of their presence as symbols rather than simply as part of the background to everyday life. It is said that Ludwig Wittgenstein observed that merely repeating a word many times and focusing on it as a word is sufficient to rob it of its meaning. In the same way, when a symbol becomes controversial, it may draw too much attention to itself to be effective as a veil.

For instance, some might see the motto "In God We Trust" as an insidious avenue to "smuggle in" references to God in defiance of a constitutional separation of religion and state. Similarly, others might charge that a veil such as the Statue of Liberty also insidiously valorizes a particular aesthetic, namely whiteness, as well as associates white women with an important value of liberty. If such complaints become common, then while these will remain symbols, they will be divisive ones rather than ones that work constructively for a liberal state.[22]

---

[22] Native Americans have registered similar complaints over the use of Andrew Jackson's image on the twenty-dollar bill. Jackson was the president who ordered

An additional consideration concerns the way that the number of symbols vying for significance and attention relates to the effectiveness of these veils. For instance, consider the sometimes emotionally charged debate over the construction of a memorial to honor the veterans of World War II. Many people argued that it was important to place the World War II Veterans monument on the Mall in order to pay proper tribute to the sacrifices of a whole generation of Americans. Others argued that while such a memorial would be appropriate, there were other compelling reasons to preserve the Mall as it is.

Of course, many different factors are relevant in a debate of this sort. In terms of the effectiveness of such a memorial, however, the crucial point is how the public will respond to it. For instance, it may simply be a psychological fact that people can grasp only a few civic exemplars at a time, which might be a reason to limit the number of memorials on the Mall. The same reasoning would support limiting President's Day to honoring just Washington and Lincoln; while other presidents might be deserving of a similar honor, expanding the pool may just dilute the intended message.

The more complicated issue is that of the legitimacy of particular liberal veils, and it is to this that the rest of this chapter is devoted. I propose that we define the legitimacy of liberal veils in terms of three factors:

1. *Content*: Is the veil one that undermines the autonomy of citizens to whom it is directed or in any other way undermines basic liberal values?
2. *Translucency*: Is it possible for interested citizens to penetrate the veil, or is it opaque?
3. *Consent*: Were the decisions regarding the use of these veils made in a way that reflects the consent of the target population?

I have already discussed (2), the condition of transparency, in Chapter 1. This essentially requires that the veil allow an interested party – but not necessarily a casual observer – to "see through" the superficial image to the true nature of the veiled object.

The other two conditions are more difficult to characterize. Condition (1) – content – focuses on the veil itself and its effects, and requires that we consider two different ways in which the veil might undermine

the removal of the Cherokee Nation from Georgia and set them on the infamous "Trail of Tears" into Oklahoma.

liberal aims. The first concerns the (contingent) effects of the veil on the population's reaction to them; if they tend to erode the liberty, freedom, and equality of citizens, they are illegitimate. The second way in which a veil may be illegitimate is related to the point raised in section 3.3, that is, that autonomy requires veils be tailored to match the target population's own culture and traditions. Imposing an alien or unfamiliar culture is liable to be ineffective in any event, but if one is successfully imposed upon a population, it is likely to undermine the autonomy of that population.

As an example of the relevant factors in this judgment, consider the recent controversy over the flying of the Confederate battle flag over the state capitol in South Carolina. The symbol in this case has been invested with radically different meanings and expectations by different people. Some see the flag as a symbol of the valor of Confederate soldiers and the skill of their military leaders. Others, however, see the very same flag as a symbol of oppression, one that symbolizes discrimination and disenfranchisement – fears well grounded in the history of slavery, Jim Crow, and racism.

Part of the complexity of this dispute stems from its being a matter of the meaning attributed to a symbol. It is further complicated by the fact that it arises from an interaction among symbols. That is, opposition to the Confederate flag is *not* opposition to the flag per se. The NAACP does not, for instance, threaten boycotts against states in which Confederate flags are displayed in museums as a historical record. Rather, opposition is geared toward stopping the flying of the flag *on a state capitol building*, a building that is itself highly symbolic, a place that is presumed to be a common space for all citizens. Flying this flag in this kind of space creates a symbol of a special kind, this time one that many take to be a sign of profound disrespect for hundreds of years of abuse. The proponents' answer has been that they want to preserve their heritage; the opponents' retort has been that *their* heritage is their excruciating, lingering pain.

As it happens, there are good reasons to think that the intention behind flying the flag was not solely to celebrate the legacy of Confederate warriors. For instance, the first time after the Civil War that civil leaders in South Carolina used the flag was at the 1948 Democratic Party national convention. The Southern delegations responded to the adoption of various civil rights planks in the party platform by waving the battle flag as they walked out of the convention in protest. The flag was also used in the 1950s as a protest against integration and progress on civil rights, while in the 1960s, South Carolina raised the Confederate flag over its capitol dome as a way both of celebrating the Civil War Centenary and as a signal of defiance over the federal court ruling against segregation.

I believe that flying the Confederate battle flag over the South Carolina capitol dome fails the legitimacy test because of its content as a symbol. First and foremost, as a symbol of those who fought on the wrong side of the slavery issue, it is clearly in conflict with the central values of liberal democracy. Second, as a representation of secession, the flag stands opposed to the most basic of civic values: the preservation of the state.

I stress, however, the completely *contingent* nature of the meaning of symbols like the Confederate flag. If, over time, the Confederate flag comes to be regarded as a symbol of gallantry – the virtue exhibited by Confederate military, rather than the racist political principles that the military was used to defend – there would be no good reason to take the flag down. For instance, the image of St. George slaying the dragon seems perfectly fine to use in a liberal democracy, since it valorizes courage and steadfastness. It would be quite another thing if it were seen as a symbol of gratuitous cruelty to reptiles.[23]

Appropriate content and translucency are not, however, sufficient to ensure that a veil will be legitimate by the liberal standards I have proposed. The concern that remains is that of manipulation, or the fear that opportunists may produce veils in order to lead others where they may not wish to go.

One way to do this is analogous to the way liberals have traditionally approached the question of the legitimacy of institutions. That is, liberal veils should be ones that either are *actually* consented to by the polity or are such that *were* they cast into light for all to see after careful deliberation, competent individuals *would* consent to them. This approach suggests two different sufficient conditions for the legitimacy of a veil:

- It is actually the product of some more-or-less democratic process, *or*
- It would have been accepted by citizens if they were to have the appropriate information and had the time, energy, and intelligence to make a reasonable judgment about it.

[23] A different kind of argument for removing the Confederate flag from the South Carolina capitol would involve showing that flying the flag has a detectable and deleterious effect on people. This argument would be analogous to those used in *Brown v. Board of Education*, which appealed to the empirical effects of segregation to argue that it was unconstitutional.

3.4. Justification for Veils

Hence, the justifications for veils follow in two complementary parts: *actual* and *hypothetical* justifications.

3.4.1. Actual Justification

Actual justification deals with existing veils and their justification. This justification calls for a case-by-case study of particular veils to see not merely whether they support liberal democratic values but also that they were arrived at via democratic processes.

For an example of a veil that is justified in this way, consider the Vietnam Veterans Memorial.[24] The idea of the Memorial was not the result of a form of fiat from the top down but grew out of a grass-roots movement subjected to broadly democratic processes during its planning and design. A private citizen and an ex-infantry corporal, Jan Scruggs, incubated the idea of the Vietnam Veteran Memorial in 1979 and founded the Vietnam Veterans Memorial Fund. The Fund sponsored an open competition for the design that attracted 1,421 submissions, and a jury of eight chose the design of Maya Lin, then a senior at Yale. Despite resistance from influential figures (including H. Ross Perot and the secretaries of the navy and the interior), the Memorial was completed, although in a compromise, a traditional statue, *The Fightingmen*, and a flagpole were added over Lin's opposition.[25,26]

The Franklin Roosevelt Memorial is another example of a veil that went through a protracted democratic debate over whether to present FDR in a wheelchair or not. Interests were represented. Handicapped

---

[24] I rely on the history of the Vietnam Veterans Memorial and the Civil Rights Memorial from an original description and historical account of Daniel Abramsom, "Maya Lin and the 1960s: Monuments, Time Lines and Minimalism," *Critical Inquiry*, Vol. 22, No. 4, (1996), p. 688.

[25] Ibid., footnote 8, p. 684. For the controversy over the Vietnam Veteran's Memorial, see Tom Garhart, "A Better Way to Honor Viet Vets," *Washington Post*, November 15, 1982, pp. B1, B6; Isabel Wilkerson, "'Art War' Erupts over Vietnam Veteran Memorial," *Washington Post*, July 8, 1982, p. D3; see Abramson, ibid, for more citations on the challenges from the general public over the Memorial.

[26] The Civil Rights Memorial had similar grassroots origins, being conceived of in 1987 by a civil rights lawyer, Morris Dees, in the wake of his realization that many young people, especially Southern blacks, knew little about the history of the civil rights movements. He said, "I saw the need of such a shrine as a way to make future generations aware of the importance of the movement" (Morris Dees, "Law Center to Build Civil Right Memorial," *Law Report of the Southern Poverty Law Center*, October 4, 1988, p. 3). Dees's organization, the Southern Poverty Law Center, provided the seed money for the sponsor of the proposed memorial.

citizens argued that he be presented on the wheelchair as a means of recognizing the handicapped, while others felt just as strongly that he should be presented as he presented himself in public – *without* a wheelchair. These issues of representations were democratically debated not only for us (here and now) but also for the future generation of citizens. These memorials were debated in the Congress before they were finally implemented.

As a final example of another veil that was subjected to public scrutiny of this sort, consider the design on the reverse side of the dollar bill. There one will find, among many things, two designs. On the left is an unfinished pyramid, its base inscribed with the date 1776 in Roman numerals: MDCCLXXVI. Atop the pyramid is a triangle with the all-seeing eye of Divine Providence, above which is etched the motto, "Annuit coeptis" ("He has smiled on our undertaking"). At the base of the pyramid is a scroll bearing the motto, "Novus ordo secclorum" ("New Order of the Ages"). On the right-hand side is an American eagle bearing on its breast a shield with thirteen narrow vertical stripes. In its talons the eagle clutches an olive branch and a cluster of thirteen arrows, and in its beak a scroll with the motto "E pluribus Unum" ("from many, one").

The Continental Congress first commissioned the design of the seal immediately after the signing of the Declaration of Independence on July 4, 1776. The design went through three committees and it took a total of six years and a combination of designs of the three committees to come out with the final design. Six years allowed enough time for democratic deliberations and debates, as indeed was necessary to reach the final design.[27]

3.4.2. *Hypothetical Justification*

In the cases discussed in the preceding section, the polity's consent to the symbols used was actual. The fact that the public had either directly or indirectly (via elected representatives) chosen the content of these symbols is sufficient to establish the legitimacy of the veil for a liberal state (granting, of course, that the other conditions obtain). But requiring this kind of actual consent for a veil's legitimacy is too stringent. Just as insisting on actual consent for laws and general institutions would sharply limit the legitimacy of any liberal state, so too would limiting

[27] I will look at the detailed history and the legitimacy of the use of other symbols in the seal in the next chapter.

legitimate liberal veils to those that (such as those discussed in the preceding section) were designed in a conscious manner. This would imply that the numerous veils that arise in other ways would automatically fail to be legitimate.

For instance, some symbols (such as flags and other national symbols) may have arisen in nonliberal systems and been invested with significance that remains even after a transition to liberalism. In such cases, there would have been no appropriate level of actual consent. Other symbols or traditions may arise within liberal systems, but in largely informal ways, without any conscious judgment, decision, or deliberation by anyone, let alone a properly transparent approval procedure. Here, too, actual consent is lacking.[28]

In important ways, the lack of actual consent helps contribute to the effectiveness of veils in shaping judgments, character, and behavior. As I have argued in Chapter 1, the effectiveness of many veils depends on their being "invisible," blending into the background. Given this, we might expect explicit deliberation over the content and design of veils to be counterproductive, at least in the short term. Public debate over veils focuses attention on its intended role and purpose, which may often be divisive. In contrast, if the veil is simply part of the way we live – something that simply has "always been this way" – it will tend to be uncontroversial and hence better serve the end of supporting particular values.

This is just another manifestation of the tension discussed in section 1.5: Legitimacy suggests actual consent, while effectiveness calls for avoiding explicit debate. The concept of *hypothetical consent* allows us to underwrite the legitimacy of these veils despite their failing to undergo the scrutiny we would typically demand in a liberal state. That is, instead of considering the actual history of the veil, we ask whether citizens would have accepted it if they were to have the appropriate information and had the time, energy, and intelligence to make a reasonable judgment about it.[29] Practical issues make it impossible to secure

---

[28] In his book *Convention: A Philosophical Study* (Cambridge, MA: Harvard University Press, 1969), David Lewis describes how some arrangements might arise without any particular conscious decision being made by any discernable individual or groups thereof. A similar phenomenon might be the way individuals' uncoordinated actions might give rise to a kind of overall coordinated system.

[29] On the surface, this may seem a bit paternalistic. However, it doesn't seem any worse in that respect than the highly indirect governance demanded in any large and complex state.

actual consent in every case. Instead, we need to ask a hypothetical question: Would citizens willingly accept the existing veils if they knew the purposes they served?

The use of this hypothetical justification is particularly apt for veils, given their multilayered nature as described in section 1.2. The practical purpose of the veil is to help provide the desired reaction in citizens when those citizens vary widely with respect to interests and abilities. In particular, some have both the desire and the capacity to engage with abstract philosophical and political principles, while many others lack one or the other of these. Veils overlay the true nature of an object or institution with a surface image intended to influence action, character, and judgment on the basis of the superficial features that would strike the casual onlooker. At the same time, these veiled objects should withstand the critical inquiry and investigation of others who take a deeper interest in them.

If only for the sake of stability, then, veiled objects should be amenable to both those who are moved only by surface images and those who penetrate the veil and see what the object really is. But this two-tiered structure of responses to veils has a natural connection to hypothetical consent. That is, we can take the reactions of those who "see through" veils to the real nature of a political institution or set of values as representative of what others *would* say if they were to do the same. If the institution is not consented to by those who see through the veils, then we can take this as a sign that the veil undermines the liberal value of autonomy and self-determination. The veil in this case makes palatable an institution that would be unacceptable to one who understands the purposes for which the veil is used.

The possibility of this kind of hypothetical justification of veils has two important effects. The first is to allow liberals to make use of veils that were *not* the product of some explicitly democratic process of design and implementation. As noted previously, veils arise in a variety of ways, and many of the symbols, motifs, themes, and rituals that play roles in modern liberal democracies today have their roots in nonliberal social organizations of the past. The circumstances of their origin, however, does not necessarily mean they cannot be put to work for liberal purposes in a way that is consistent with liberal principles.

The second effect of this justification complements the first, and allows us to criticize the use of particular veils even though there is little or no actual resistance to them. As I stressed in section 3.1, the use of veils is often rightly viewed with suspicion. What I have focused on in section 3.1 is their effectiveness in shaping character and action. In addition to being effective means, however, the way they operate on the emotions makes changing them very difficult and liable to spark intense resistance. As Michael Walzer has observed:

> They [symbols or veils] shape our whole sensibility; they guarantee a sure place in a known world; they tell us more than we easily repeat. And so their transformation encounters a resistance which logical demonstration does not or ought not to meet.[30]

The possibility of abuse of veils, together with the difficulties that arise when we try to remove an entrenched but illegitimate veil, makes it important to have a way to identify illegitimate veils and to undermine their symbolic power.

With respect to the problem of identifying illegitimate veils, it is not enough to assume that citizens will notice and complain about them. Much of the power of veils lies in their being part of everyday life; it is their ubiquity and seamless integration into what we take for granted that allows them to shape how we live.

How should we identify these abuses? Ideally, we might count on the diversity and independence of individuals in a liberal society to do the work. That is, we might assume that if there is no general challenge to a veil from within a well-ordered liberal democracy, then the *absence* of protest can be a signal of prima facie justification for veils. An example is the numismatic symbols. I would claim that the use of portraits of civic heroes on U.S. coins and currency is a legitimate use of veils; they tell particular narratives about the United States and create a sense of cohesion by promoting civic heroism.

More controversial, perhaps, is the fact that those same coins and pieces of currency contain the phrase "In God We Trust," which some claim violates the separation of church and state. While there are some who make this charge, this opposition to references to God on money is fairly weak; more citizens in the United States would probably be disturbed by efforts to remove the motto than are troubled by its existence. If mere absence of protest implied that the veil was legitimate, then there are no grounds for removing this veil or replacing it with something (perhaps) less offensive, such as "In Science and Secular Progress We Trust."

---

[30] Michael Walzer, "On the Role of Symbolism in Political Thought," *Political Science Quarterly*, Vol. 82, No. 2 (1967), p. 198.

From a practical point of view, there may be excellent reasons to tolerate veils that constitute technical violations of liberal principles. Regarding the issue of governmental references to a deity, for instance, Sandford Levinson claims that "In God we Trust" on the coinage is unconstitutional government speech. At the same time, however, he warns of the dangers of meddling with such symbols: "Judicial caution is especially merited when the challenged practices have become sedimented in historical memory and simply accepted as a *status quo.*"[31] The upshot of this seems to be that while veils of this kind (and others, such as Christian symbols in the "public square") violate the letter of liberal principles, they may be so firmly entrenched in the imagination and memory of citizens that rooting them out will either be fruitless or more harmful to the community than the original offense.

This view acknowledges the basic tension between fundamental liberal values and the means of achieving the political stability needed to implement those values. It also acknowledges that the mere absence of complaints about a veil is *not* sufficient to show that it is not abusive – a point that is all the more obvious to those who recognize the power of veils and the way they work. After all, one of the features of veils that make them so useful for liberal democratic (and non-liberal, non-democratic) purposes is that they circumvent conscious thought processes. They are in many cases so deeply engrained in our lives that they are invisible, to say the least, yet they exert an influence on how we think and behave.[32]

Appreciating the way that such unobtrusive factors can affect our judgments helps to undermine the claim that a veil is legitimate if it doesn't raise or rouse complaints and protests. Well-functioning veils won't draw attention to themselves anyway – and it seems implausible to think that only legitimate veils will be useful in this respect. In fact, some of the most dangerous veils (from the liberal democratic point of view) may be ones that no one notices, in which case we *shouldn't* infer that they are legitimate from the mere fact that they are not discerned.

---

[31] Sanford Levinson, *Written in Stone* (Durham, NC: Duke University Press, 1998), p. 105.

[32] Think of the historical use of the masculine pronoun *he* and *his* or *mankind* as a kind of generic term. Many people find this perfectly natural – and find a similar use of *she* or *her* (particularly when referring to God) jarring or even divisive. Picking a single gender to use for generic references of this sort may be harmless, but it may also have troubling effects on attitudes about men and women.

Appealing to a hypothetical justification gives us a position from which we can see that an apparently innocuous veil is in fact unacceptable for liberals. A critical assessment of veils requires that we ask what an informed and interested citizen would conclude if the veil were to be lifted and the object – the values, practices, or institutions being veiled – were revealed.

3.5. CONCLUSION

One of the fundamental values of liberal states is the autonomy of citizens. There is room for much philosophical debate over the exact nature of autonomy. One extreme view envisions the autonomous individual as unburdened by a history; a set of traditions – a collection of culturally based beliefs, intuitions, and practices – is of limited value. If this is what autonomy requires, then I cannot see how any political system could hope to approach, let alone achieve, this goal.

Despite its impracticality, this lofty ideal of autonomy seems to capture one important fact: The autonomous agent lives her life "from the inside," as it were. The autonomous agent acts for reasons and causes that are, in an important sense, *her own*. On the extreme view of autonomy, tradition and culture are assumed to be external to the individual; insofar as agents are moved by those forces, they lack autonomy. The fundamental difference between this extreme view of autonomy and the tradition-based approach I have presented in section 3.3 is that I believe there is a clear sense in which social and cultural forces can be internalized in a way that can give individual "ownership." The fact that the cause of my action or choice is a cultural force or a tradition does not necessarily rob me of autonomy; what is crucial is whether that culture or tradition is *my own*.

Given this general view of autonomy, we can begin to discern the role and justification of political veils in a liberal state. Most significantly, this view allows us to see why the argument for veil politics does not commit one to *all* veils. The conditions outlined in section 3.4 provide criteria by which we can separate those veils that *are* appropriate for a liberal state from those that are not.

Recognizing how we can use veils for liberal purposes is not just an academic point, but one that has important practical effects. Failing to realize the role of veils puts liberals at a disadvantage by risking the weakening of citizens' belief in the fundamental values or leaving the central political artery of motivation to luck. Procuring, preserving, and advancing freedom in liberal democratic states is too serious a matter to be left to chance or some superstition such as Adam Smith's "unseen hand." Political arrangements are not like the planets in their orbits that, once on their path, do not collide with each other; nor are they like trees that once planted grow while people sleep. They are like machines that need to be tuned, oiled, and fueled even when they are in good working condition, and repaired when they are falling apart. I do not doubt the utility of fortune, but by its very nature, there is no guarantee that it will continue. Veils close the gap of fortune and make liberal democratic arrangement our own artifact.

Such being the case, we must be ready to answer questions about the political order as well as social arrangements that will ensure the continuity of the state. On the one hand, liberal states need the externalization of individuals' internal convictions, and on the other, they need the internalization of some prescribed external convictions to make the former possible. A well-ordered state cannot exist for more than a short time if its members do not observe common basic ways of behavior. This implies that the state must take measures to adjust certain actions, desires, and styles of life to the common social denominator necessary for freedom to be possible in the first place.

Chapter 4

The Art of Liberal Politics

In Chapter 3 I argued that there is no principled reason to think that liberals cannot practice veil politics – the intentional use and manipulation of veils for political purposes. There I discussed the relationship between autonomy and an agent's own culture and history, and argued that the intimate connection between these factors opens the way for using veils for liberal purposes. This relationship also imposes special restrictions on how liberals can use veils. As laid out in section 3.4, relevant considerations include the notions of appropriate liberal content, translucency of veils, and some degree of consent (either actual or hypothetical) by the population to the veils.

The aim of this chapter is to add details to how a liberal version of veil politics can be implemented. That is, given the general theoretical understanding of the structure and function of veils (as presented in Chapters 1 and 2), and an account of the conditions under which a veil would be consistent with liberal principles (Chapter 3), we now turn to the practical problems of the art of politics – the issues that arise in using veil politics to create and sustain a liberal political structure.[1]

A salient feature of liberal democracies is that they are citizen-based; government in such states is, as intoned by Lincoln, "of the people, by the people, and for the people." Implicit in this understanding of liberal states as citizen-based is the requirement that state officials have no monopoly on the design, control, and application of veils as means of motivation and communication. This condition affects both the kind of content that is allowed in legitimate liberal veils and the extent to which the public may be said to have consented to those veils. Altering

---

[1] Chapter 5 extends this practical aim, and focuses on programs of civic education that incorporate uses of veils.

73

the meaning and significance of veils in more-or-less dramatic ways, then, should be something of which citizens in a liberal democracy are capable – and in part, guarantees of freedom of speech and expression help to make this possible.

This chapter will focus on this issue of participation in the definition, application, and redefinition of veils. In sections 4.1 and 4.2, I examine various degrees to which citizens can fail or succeed in being able to participate in the use and development of veils, and link the degree of participation in a given society with the conditions of content and consent outlined previously. When the public becomes more active in defining the symbolic features of their political community, those features are more likely to be expressions of the character and culture of the people of that community, which I have argued (in section 3.3) is a condition of autonomy. At the same time, just as high levels of participation in the political process (such as voting, following public policy debates, and so on) constitute evidence for consent for the state's policies, so too participation with respect to veils indicates consent to the use of veils and, ultimately, to the institutions and processes being veiled.

Finally, in the last part of this chapter I illustrate some of the complexities involved in participation by looking at how one particular civic narrative, centered on the Declaration of Independence, has been shaped and redefined in various ways by the active participation of various parties – some of whom were members of the political elite, while (more surprisingly) others were actually among the disenfranchised.

4.1. NONPARTICIPATORY REGIMES

There is something especially terrifying by the prospect of a citizenry controlled and manipulated not by brute force, but by the mysterious force of veils appropriated and controlled by a political elite or state. This monopolistic control of veils is what I described in Chapter 1 as opacity politics, a style of political practice in which states of affairs regarding political institutions and practices are hidden or rendered invisible from the general public.[2]

---

[2] One of my main aims is to show that there is no necessary connection between veil politics and any particular set of political values. Specifically, the intentional use of veils for political purposes does *not* require rejecting liberalism, nor, for that matter, does rejecting liberalism imply automatically that one must practice veil politics; some repressive and brutal states have been quite open about the nature of their illiberal institutions and in that sense are models of transparency. Since there are

4.1. Nonparticipatory Regimes

In this section, I will take a closer look at the notion of opaque veils – particularly with respect to the connection between opacity and the ability of the general population (rather than just the political elites) to participate in shaping and altering political veils. On the view I shall present, there is an intimate link between participation in this sense and the legitimacy of veils. I also lay out three kinds of regimes in which this kind of participation is denied: *manipulative regimes, pure mythic regimes,* and *colonized regimes*. In this section I describe each of these in turn; in section 4.2 I will contrast them with what I refer to as *participatory veil regimes* or *liberal democratic regimes*.

The distinctions drawn in the following sections between pure mythic, manipulative, and colonized regimes are given in terms of *who* constructs or controls these opaque veils. At one end of the spectrum are pure mythic regimes, in which the meaning of veils is entirely inherited – no agent who acts within the system controls the meaning or significance of symbols in any conscious manner. At the other end of the spectrum are manipulative regimes, which are ones in which opaque veils are deliberately either constructed or deployed for particular political purposes. In between are colonized regimes, in which intermediate levels of deliberate control are exercised. In each of these regimes, however, the meaning and significance associated with political veils is out of the control of the general public.

There are three important reasons for taking this closer look at opaque political regimes. The first of these is to flesh out the notions of opacity and translucency. As introduced in Chapter 1, opaque veils are simply ones that in some way resist being penetrated. But what does this mean? If translucency is a condition for liberal veils, what kinds of evidence might we use to discriminate between opaque and translucent veils? As in most interesting distinctions, there is no absolutely clear distinction between translucency and opacity. However, by looking at different kinds of opaque regimes, we will be able to develop a more detailed profile of opaque veils.

The second reason is that it allows us to see different ways that opaque veils may fail to satisfy the conditions required of legitimate liberal veils.

more and less effective combinations of principles and modes of practice, however, there may be particular correlations. For instance, genuine "Machiavellian horrors" are features that are best veiled; naked force may succeed in stopping resistance to such horrors, but a more effective tactic may be to cover them in some way. Thus, there may be a natural tendency in oppressive states toward opacity politics.

Specifically, the examples I will consider indicate a natural link between the use of opaque veils and certain kinds of nonliberal regimes. In that sense, we can see a significant relationship between the features of a political system and the types of veils appropriate or most effective relative to that system.

A third reason to examine opaque regimes is to reveal a particular kind of threat posed by the failure of translucency. In particular, I argue that what we typically find in regimes of these sorts is a breakdown in the value assigned to individuals and individuality. Opaque veils, that is, tend to foster a kind of collectivist attitude, a reduction of individuals that I shall call a *massdom*. This is a polity in which the multitude of independent factors whose interactions are normally responsible for investing and altering the meanings of symbols are replaced or significantly coopted by a single factor that has the potential to move everyone to perform mindless actions. In order to control individuals, narratives are compressed, concentrated, and embodied in the leadership who – with the help of the underlying customs, religious, and spiritual doctrines that support the basic structure of the society – control both the production and use of veils in motivating citizens. In this state of affairs, respect and reverence are directed to the supreme leader of the state rather than (as is the case of most liberal democracies) to impersonal institutions, principles, ideals, or creeds.

Understanding this risk that comes with the use of opaque veils is important when we consider putting veil politics into practice. Again, my interest is not simply in giving a theoretical analysis of how symbols are used in states with particular kinds of structures, but in providing a framework for political practice. By understanding the way veils can be abused, we learn ways to introduce checks on the deliberate use of veils that will allow us to use them effectively for liberal purposes *without* violating basic liberal principles.

4.1.1. Manipulative Regimes

As noted previously, the distinctions I will be drawing among different kinds of opaque regimes are in terms of what we might call the deliberate control these regimes have over political veils. In each, the devices used to adorn or "cover" political processes, institutions, and arrangements are opaque, that is, they are ones that resist efforts to see through them to the true nature of the object being veiled. Where they differ is the extent to which members of the community can manipulate the meanings (and hence, the effects) of these veils.

The basic idea of an opaque regime is one that veils political institutions in ways that resist being penetrated. In those terms, it is natural to identify an opaque regime with those in which veils are explicitly designed to resist every effort to penetrate them, and where force of some kind is used to deal with those who attempt to reveal the true nature of the state's structure and organization. These kinds of states are what I will refer to as *manipulative* regimes – where manipulation should be taken to imply deliberate design and use of opaque veils.

As a highly idealized image of a manipulative regime, imagine a state in which a few individuals (either elected or self-appointed) produce veils for the purpose of hiding from citizens the true nature of political institutions and practices because those institutions and practices are too awful to stand the light of the day.[3] Revealing their true nature, in other words, would undermine whatever allegiance citizens would feel toward the state, making it imperative that those in charge of the veils block efforts to look beyond those veils. Clever design of veils – ones that take advantage of a thorough understanding of the existing traditions, habits, and customs of the population – is one way to guard against the truth being revealed. If that fails, of course, there is always brute force.

The thinker associated with using image to prop up regimes that, if taken from the shadows into the light, would never garner the consent of the public is the great political observer, Machiavelli. In what I consider a sixteenth century handbook to opacity politics, *The Prince*, Machiavelli affirms that morality, religion, and customs had a place in politics only as means to be appropriated and deployed by the prince to acquire and keep power for himself.

This cynical use of moral and religious convictions would, of course, hardly be effective if it were seen simply as a means of manipulating the public. It is not surprising, then, to find that Machiavelli authored *The Prince* as a secret counsel to Florentine's prince, Lorenzo de Medici, on how to obtain and maintain power by using these means of persuading the citizenry. The advice intended to help the prince succeed in this

---

[3] Note that the awfulness of political institutions is only one reason why they would have to be veiled. Another possibility is that, stripped of their adornments, those institutions would fail to inspire citizens to participate in the manner required for the proper working of the state. That is, in oppressive states, the horrors need to be veiled in order to maintain a stable, working state; in non-oppressive states, it may be the ordinariness of political institutions that may have to be veiled.

objective were supposed to be kept secret from the citizens. When deployed by the prince, they were to have the effects on citizens of the *arcana imperii* (or mysteries of state) because Machiavelli knew that the knowledge of the authorship of veils could create resentment from the people.

There are good reasons to think that opacity to this extreme degree is, while in principle possible, perhaps impossible in practice today. Given the myriad sources of information available today even where the media is state-controlled, none but the most repressive states would be capable of exerting a monopolistic control over information available to individuals.

Historically, however, states *have* been able to exercise significant control over not just media sources but over the image of the state in the minds of its citizens. The example that leaps to mind is that of Hitler's sophisticated propaganda machine. As implemented by Joseph Goebbels and others, the Nazi propaganda campaign systematically tapped into the established cultural, ethnic, and national symbols of the German people to construct an image that, for many in the population being "targeted," was a compelling one.

In the process of building up a set of images associated with the Nazi regime, the Nazis appropriated a hodge-podge of tribal and ethnic stories, forged from them a general myth of the Aryan race, and set it against *another* fabricated race, the Jews, the supposed source of the purer German race's miseries. The Aryan ideal was linked to Teutonic heroes and represented in the cult of the body, celebrating youth and vitality; the Jew, on the other hand, was represented as occupying a middle ground between man and beast by Nazi science.

These are images as powerful as they are reprehensible. The Nazi propagandist flattered a people who were humiliated by their defeat in World War I and their treatment in the aftermath of that war. By setting up Jews as scapegoats, they played to an entrenched tradition of anti-Semitism that *already* regarded Jews as suspicious. Finally, in systematically and persistently fostering sharply defined types with clear-cut adversarial relationships – Aryan versus Jew, Christian versus communist, patriot versus foreigner – the Nazi propagandist had a framework that made up for its lack of verisimilitude in its ability to capture the imagination of a relatively sophisticated and well-educated German population.

The evil genius of the Nazis is that they aestheticized and invested these messages in narratives, liturgies, ceremonies, uniforms, architectural designs, games, songs, and gestures. Of special note here were the Nazis' commissioned movies, *Triumph of the Will* and *Olympia*, both directed by Leni Riefenstahl. On the face of it, the movies were exceptional works of art; *Olympia* won the top prize at the 1938 Venice Film Festival (appropriately called the Mussolini Cup). In fact, however, these were pieces of political art, celebrations of the resurgent Reich and the ideals of the physical beauty and power of German youth.

The Nazi regime vividly illustrates the threat of state monopoly over the production and deployment of opaque veils, and represents the terrible synthesis of Machiavelli's political style with modern media technology.[4] As Ernst Cassirer observed,

The Twentieth century developed a *technique* of mythical thought which had no equal in previous history. Henceforth myths were invented and manufactured in the same sense and according to the same methods as machine guns or airplanes. And they were used for the same purpose, for internal and external warfare. This was an altogether unprecedented fact, a fact which has changed the whole face of our modern political life.[5]

As modern technology multiplies the power and efficiency of weapons, the ability of modern states to control media makes it possible for it to create and disseminate a single historical narrative. In extreme cases, this may amount to creating a wholly self-serving retelling of history shared by all citizens; in other cases, the influence may be more subtle, with a centralized authority "feeding" independent sources (such as media outlets) information intended to present a particular public image.[6]

While oppressive states like Nazi Germany and Stalin's Soviet Union are perhaps the most obvious examples of manipulative regimes, it is important to note that the opacity of veils and their use in manipulation is in principle independent of the content of the aims of the political system they are used to support. It may be the rule that manipulative regimes are devoted to the enrichment of the political elite – the *manipulators* – but it may also be that the intended beneficiaries are those who are *manipulated*. There may be, then, benevolent manipulative regimes,

[4] Max Weber has defined the state as an organization with monopoly over the use of force. In a similar way, we can think of a manipulative opaque state as one with a monopoly over the meaning and use of political veils.

[5] Ernst Cassirer, *Symbol, Myth, and Culture: Essays and Lectures of Ernst Cassirer 1935–1945*, ed. Donald P. Verene (New Haven, CT: Yale University Press, 1979), p. 253.

[6] See, for instance, Edward Herman and Noam Chomsky's *Manufacturing Consent: The Political Economy of the Mass Media* (New York: Pantheon Books, 2002) for a version of this view.

ones that hold to the "reason of state doctrine" that justifies deception and the manipulation of customs, religion, and even extralegal force for the public good. The philosopher-king envisioned by Plato in his *Republic* is an example of a proposed benevolent manipulative regime that uses opaque myths and fabrications for the good of the general population. In at least popular views of history, there is a concept of "enlightened despots" – Catherine and Peter of Russia, Frederick the Great of Prussia, Joseph II of Austria, and, more recently, Nwalima Julius Nyerere of Tanzania. The benign reputations of these rulers may or may not be deserved, but at least suggest that in principle, the methods of manipulative opacity politics may be put to use for the benefit of those being manipulated.[7]

4.1.2. *Pure Mythic Regimes*

In the preceding section, I have described one type of opaque regime, and have argued that the possibility of benevolent manipulative regimes shows that opacity is not essentially linked to malevolent purposes.[8] Opacity, then, describes a *style* of governance, not the content of a state's political principles or ideals.

Just as the opacity of a regime tells us little about the principles and aims of that state, so too the fact that a state is opaque does not imply that it is manipulative in the sense described in the preceding section. That is, in manipulative regimes, agents are *deliberately* engaged in the art of myth-making for the sake of gaining and keeping power. To that end, the veils are intentionally designed to resist penetration, and physical force or intimidation may be used to prevent the true nature of veiled objects from being brought to light. In what I refer to as *purely mythic regimes*, however, opacity is not an intentional feature of political veils,

---

[7] These reputations may themselves be sentimental reworkings of history for present political purposes. The very idea of an enlightened despot may, like the images of icons like Lincoln and the founders described in section 1.1, be nothing more than two-dimensional, literally false representations used to highlight particular values and ideals.

[8] Given particular views of what constitutes benign states, opacity may imply judgments about the benevolent or malevolent status of a state. For instance, many would regard mere manipulation – even for liberal purposes – as malevolent, a denial of autonomy or self-determination. That is one of the reasons for including the requirement of transparency in the conditions for liberal veils given in section 3.4.

but rather arises from a widespread naïve view of the sources of the meaning and significance of symbols, traditions, and rituals.

One way of thinking of pure opacity regimes is to think of ones in which no one – not even the political elite – penetrates veils. In such regimes, traditions and symbols that play a role in social organization will, of course, have significance and meaning, but these are not determined by *conscious* efforts to create symbols for particular purposes or to appropriate existing symbols for political ends. If asked for a source of a ritual's significance or importance, for instance, no member of such a community could do better than to make a vague reference to the past, perhaps "our ancestors."[9]

If we think of veils in terms of Plato's "noble lie" – a deception intentionally devised by the elite for the purpose of controlling those they rule – a veil in a pure mythic regime would be, in Plato's words, "some magnificent myth that would in itself carry conviction to our whole community," where the reference to the "whole community" is taken quite literally, encompassing both the ruling elite and the ruled. Such a myth comes from nowhere and no one in particular, and in many ways its believability is enhanced by its vagueness.[10]

As noted previously, purely mythic regimes require a rather naïve attitude toward the origins of traditions and symbols. In such states, questions about why we should revere particular figures or institutions simply do not arise, which is a level of complacency that (for many self-conscious inhabitants of liberal states, at least) is hard to imagine is possible today. Maintaining this level of naivety in a world filled with people who challenge traditions of this sort would require a degree of isolation almost unimaginable today.

---

[9] To claim that the meanings of veils in pure mythic regimes are assumed to be given, rather than the product of human decision, is *not* to say that these meanings are static and fixed throughout time. On the contrary, as in virtually any community, the meaning attached to particular veils will shift over time in response to changes of circumstances. However, such changes shouldn't be seen as the result of deliberate change in policy. They more closely resemble changes in slang terms or accepted standards of etiquette; like these, the meanings of veils tend to "drift" over time, but not as the result of any particular individual's decision to change the status quo.

[10] Plato remarked that such an "opportune falsehood" need be "Nothing new – a fairy story like those the poets tell and have persuaded people to believe about the sort of thing that often happened 'once upon a time,' but never does now and is not likely to [happen again]" (*Republic IV*, 414c).

Still, it is worth noting the possibility of such states as a way of underscoring the various ways in which veils may become opaque. That is, there is certainly no a priori or necessary reason to think that this attitude toward the origins of the meanings of veils makes those veils impermeable – many examples of social, political, and scientific change are essentially episodes in which beliefs that were long considered inherited "commonsense" were challenged and replaced. Once challenged, many of these otherwise resilient traditions and beliefs toppled quite easily.

The fact that some veils resist penetration, then, is not necessarily due to their having some special "intrinsic" quality. Instead, their opacity may be due to their operating in circumstances in which no one even thinks to challenge them. This underscores a general point about the way we should think about veils: The effects of a given veil depend on particular features of the community in which it functions, and this is a *contingent* matter. In that sense, the claims we make about the likely effects and (ultimately) the legitimacy of a particular kind of veil must take into consideration facts about the context in which it is applied.

In light of this, we shouldn't expect there to be a perfectly general way of gauging how easy it is to see through a particular veil. However, it seems plausible to believe that this attitude toward the origins of veils has a natural tendency to stifle interest in the real nature of political institutions – or, perhaps more accurately, such an attitude makes it difficult even to imagine a difference between the façade and the deep nature of the institution. Since this ability to draw a conceptual distinction between the object and its appearance seems to be a prerequisite of trying to look beyond appearances, this naïve attitude toward political institutions can be seen as a way of generating opacity. Nothing in the content of the veil implies that it resists efforts to penetrate it; rather, the veil's opacity is due to the population's having a particularly naïve view of meaningfulness.

4.1.3. Colonized Regimes

What unites manipulative and purely mythic regimes is the lack of control that the general population has over the meaning and use of veils. In the former, the elite of the society controls these, while in the latter it is historical contingency that has the "final word."

It is plausible to think that every state has aspects of both manipulative and pure mythic regimes. Insofar as the elites lie to the public – for reasons either malevolent or benevolent – knowing that the policy or practice being misrepresented would be unacceptable to the public, the elites are acting as a manipulative regime would. Insofar as particular veils (traditions, images, or myths) are uncritically accepted en masse by both the elites and the public, the regime qualifies as a purely mythic one.

We should expect that any state will contain elements of each of these nonparticipatory regimes. At the same time, however, there are reasons to expect that few states today will fall completely into either of these categories. As noted previously, the degree of control over the everyday lives and the information available to citizens suggests that extremely manipulative regimes are possible in only very specific (and, we might hope, ever-rarer) conditions. Similarly, we should expect pure mythic regimes to be even rarer, since the naiveté required for the members of such a state seems almost unimaginable in a world of rapid transportation and communication.

There is, however, a third class of nonparticipatory regimes that is of more pressing practical importance – what I refer to as *colonized regimes*. These represent a distinct category of states in which the governed effectively "lose control" over veils, neither by overt manipulation nor by excessive naiveté, but rather by virtue of veils imposed from outside.

I refer to these as colonized regimes to reflect the fact that for the most part these states are those in the developing world that are the products of Western colonialism.[11] Unlike manipulative regimes, they do not oppressively restrict information in any direct or indirect way. On the contrary, these states are generally open to the community of nations (especially their former colonial masters) – they trade, take loans, and buy military hardware from Western nations. Their citizens have access to the rest of the world through media like the BBC or Voice of America, and the ruling class is largely indifferent to citizens' use of other media like the Internet. However, veils in colonized regimes are not simply

---

[11] A history of colonization is not, however, necessary for colonial regimes. For instance, in his "The Clash of Civilizations?" (*Foreign Affairs*, Vol. 72, No. 3, Summer 1993, pp. 43–5), Samuel Huntington refers to "torn countries," in which the population is divided with respect to the most general level of cultural and social traditions. Huntington cites Turkey, Mexico, and Russia in the early 1990s as examples. In each, the population was divided between advocates of a modern, liberalized, and secular state and those backing a more traditionalist (or, in the case of Turkey, Islamic) state. I see this as a particular case of colonized regimes in which significant portions of the population are not engaged by the veils employed by the state.

and naively accepted from the past. Instead, these states consciously appropriate them from Western democracies, perhaps because of the influence of Western media or because many of their political elites were educated there.

That veils would be appropriated for use in politics shouldn't be a surprise. Effective veils often predate their explicitly political use, for typically it is the history of a symbol or tradition rather than its formal appearance or structure that gives it its motivational power. In colonized regimes, however, these appropriated veils are ones whose history is *not* connected to that of the citizenry in a way that would help to support liberal democratic institutions. These veils surely have a history, perhaps even one that gives them considerable motivational power with respect to citizens in the states from which they have been "transplanted"; they may be central components in the culture of liberal democracy that has taken root in other states. Merely transplanting these veils from one state to another, however, in no way guarantees – or even makes *likely* – that those veils will have the same effects in their new environment that they did in their "native" state.

Consider, for instance, regimes in the process of democratizing. The political elites of such states might naturally (and with the best of intentions) model their institutions on those of established Western democracies, sometimes to the point of mimicking not just the structure of political institutions and formal guarantees of rights and protections, but also what might be considered more superficial features of institutions.

For instance, it is usually the case that major political parties in established liberal democracies like the United States and the United Kingdom are defined in terms of ideological or economic interests rather than race, ethnicity, or religion.[12] It is not surprising, then, to find in the 1999 Nigerian constitution an explicit prohibition on all references to ethnicity and religious affiliation, not just in the official charter of a political party, but also (in obvious recognition of the power and influence of veils) in any of the party's symbols or logos.[13]

---

[12] There may be very strong correlations between ethnic or religious background and the support of a particular party as, for instance between African Americans and the Democratic Party or Protestant fundamentalists and the Republican Party in the United States. However, these correlations are likely the result of non-ethnic, non-religious factors that themselves happen to be correlated with ethnicity or religion.

[13] See Chapter 6, sections 222–3 of the 1999 Nigerian constitution; see also section 55(c) of the constitution of Ghana for a similar restriction on the content of symbols.

Since many institutions in these states are modeled on those of established liberal states, they afford many of the formal protections as those found in more established liberal states; people have the right to go to the streets and protest state action, organize new political parties, practice their religion, and enjoy the same formal protections that many in the West do. The tripartite division of the government into the executive, the judiciary, and the legislative is found in these countries (along with the advantages and disadvantages that come with those checks and balances). There are limits to holding office, elections are conducted, and respect for the United Nations Charter is written into their constitutions.

But while these rights and protections are part of the *formal* framework of the state, the types of institutions used to protect and ensure that those rights are respected are often totally alien to the citizenry, and this fact often has significant implications for how effective and stable such a state will be. In the appropriate conditions, the formal structure of an institution can have an important impact on effectiveness and stability. For instance, indirect representation and the division of government into largely autonomous executive, legislative, and judicial branches may tend to increase the stability of a state by slowing change, effectively turning revolutionary impulses into reforming ones.[14]

But the key to realizing the potential of these structures is to use them in the appropriate conditions. Placed in a society in which citizens lack a basic internalized respect for law and order, the most carefully crafted liberal institutions imaginable will probably fail. Keeping these institutions operable requires a high degree of cooperation from citizens; in effect, members of the state – both the political elite and the common citizen – must be self-policing, in the sense that they take the fact that judgments and policies have been arrived at by those institutions as sufficient motivation to obey them.

Turning the dictates of institutions into ones that citizens automatically treat as imperatives with motivating force is not something that can be achieved merely by fiat. Typically, it is a matter of a complex

---

This is not to say that these conditions were imposed *simply* on the model of established political parties; there are other, independent reasons to think that removing ethnic and religious bases from political parties might be desirable.

[14] At the same time, of course, these features may undermine effectiveness by retarding the ability of these states to respond quickly and decisively to rapid changes.

historical process in which an institution comes to occupy a special place in the civic lives of citizens. Over time, resistance to particular institutions can become practically unthinkable – with perhaps the most obvious case being that of the evolution of the status of the U.S. Supreme Court.

The Court's greatest power – that of serving as the final word in matters of constitutionality – was not formally granted by the Constitution, but rather was in a sense appropriated by John Marshall's brilliant decision in *Marbury v. Madison*.[15] More than forty years after its creation, the Supreme Court could still be mocked by Andrew Jackson who, voicing his displeasure at the Supreme Court's decision invalidating the removal of the Cherokee Nation from Georgia, said "[Chief Justice] John Marshall has made his decision; let him enforce it now if he can." Today, Supreme Court decisions are often criticized by private citizens and public officials, but there is no serious question as to their binding nature and imperative force. Only a particularly inept American politician *today* would openly make the defiant statement Jackson made in 1832.[16]

Merely introducing these institutions veiled as they were in their original setting, then, cannot be expected to generate the same results in their new environment. Instead, what may typically happen is that the institutions are set up, but are incapable of engaging citizens. The rights and protections are there in a formal sense, as are the opportunities for citizens to control their own political, social, and economic destinies. Yet, because these institutions are veiled in unfamiliar ways, they generate no genuine commitment from the people, and their potential effects are left unrealized. If the state is able to hold together, it is either because it has become largely irrelevant to the everyday lives of citizens (who may find tribal, ethnic, or other structures far more relevant), or has become oppressive.

---

[15] For discussion of this case and its implications, see George L. Haskins and Herbert A. Johnson's *Foundations of Power: John Marshall, 1801–1815* (New York: Macmillan, 1981) and Donald O. Dewey's *Marshall v. Jefferson: The Political Background of Marbury v. Madison* (New York: Knopf, 1970). For a conservative criticism of this usurpation of power, see Willmoore Kendall and George W. Carey, *The Basic Symbols of the American Political Tradition* (Baton Rouge, LA: LSU Press, 1970), pp. 138–43.

[16] The negative reaction to Franklin Roosevelt's 1937 proposal to overcome Supreme Court resistance to his New Deal programs by adding justices to the original nine – presumably just enough to give him a majority – is another example of the power that this institution has attained.

4.2. PARTICIPATORY REGIMES

In liberal democracies, persuasion rather than coercion is the primary means by which social activity is coordinated. Penal threats and the use and the threat of the use of force notwithstanding, the politics of policy making in liberal democracies is conducted mostly by getting individuals who may initially resist the policy to accept it *without* having to use force.

The regimes discussed in section 4.1 employ veils for this purpose, using them to support not just particular policies and decisions, but a general sense of cohesion of the citizenry, acceptance of the basic legitimacy of the state, and loyalty to the regime's institutions. In that respect, they are no different from liberal states, which supplement explicit argumentation and appeals to rational self-interest with appeals to a rich network of symbols and traditions to help persuade and motivate citizens.

Despite this important similarity, however, the style of politics typically practiced in these states is markedly different from that practiced in liberal democracies. In particular, the principles of liberal democracies demand an unusually high level of participation from citizens. Indeed, a fair definition of democracy is due to Joseph Schumpeter, who characterized it in terms of *democratic method*: "that institutional arrangement for arriving at political decisions in which individuals acquire the power to decide by means of a competitive struggle for the people's vote."[17]

On this procedural point of view, the essential quality of all democracies is the participation of citizens in the competitive process of determining political decisions. This leaves out explicit reference to aims, ideals, and values. As such, liberal democracies emerge as a special case of democracies, distinguished by their particular concern for the autonomy, self-respect, and equality of its citizens.[18] As a means of realizing these special liberal values, liberal democracies also demand a special kind of participation with respect to veils – specifically, they require a high level of participation in the use and definition of veils.

---

[17] *Capitalism, Socialism, and Democracy*, 2nd edition (New York: Harper, 1947), p. 269.
[18] This distinction between the notions of democracy and liberalism is clearly drawn in Isaiah Berlin's "Two Concepts of Liberty" (pp. 129–30) in *Four Essays on Liberty* (Oxford, UK: Oxford University Press, 1969) and is implicit in Samuel Huntington's *The Third Wave: Democratization in the Late Twentieth Century* (Norman, OK: University of Oklahoma Press, 1991). It is also the main theme of Fareed Zakaria's "The Rise of Illiberal Democracy," *Foreign Affairs*, Vol. 76, No. 6 (November/December 1997), pp. 22–43.

Why link participation in defining, deploying, and redefining veils to liberal democracies? One reason is that this kind of participation is intimately linked to the translucency of liberal veils. In the preceding section I have discussed some of the ways in which veils can fail one of the basic conditions of acceptable liberal veils. That is, they may fail to be translucent either because:

1. Veils are explicitly designed to be opaque, and force is used (or threatened) to maintain this opacity.
2. The population has a particularly naïve view of the source and significance of their symbols and traditions.
3. Unfamiliar veils are impressed upon a population that is unable to use them in an effective way.

In each of these cases, citizens are cut off from the veiled objects, either by (1) conscious design, (2) their own limitations, or (3) the alien nature of the veils with which they are confronted. In each of these cases, the general public is unable to participate actively in the process of defining, deploying, and redefining veils, and it is this that contributes to the opacity of veils in these regimes. I have argued (in section 3.4) that one *necessary* condition for an acceptable liberal veil is that it be translucent rather than opaque. Allowing the public the ability to participate in the use and construction of veils is one way to promote this necessary condition.

A second reason is connected to the conditions (laid out in section 3.3) that must be met for veils to support rather than to undermine autonomy. There I argued for a view of autonomy that could accommodate the obvious fact that persons live in and to a great degree are products of particular circumstances and conditions. On the sketch of such an account, there is an intimate connection between the autonomy of the members of a community and that community's having its *own* culture – including (but not limited to) its own network of symbols, customs, and traditions.

From this perspective, it is easy to see that some nonparticipatory regimes (particularly colonized ones) pose a threat to the autonomy of citizens. By imposing unfamiliar veils, these regimes first of all are liable to face practical problems. Unfamiliar veils are likely to be ineffectual veils, ones that simply have no connection to the people at whom they are directed. If, however, *that* problem doesn't arise, problems for autonomy may, for by importing what is basically an alien network of symbols and traditions, the existing network may be displaced and in turn undermine the autonomy of the "target" population.

The links between nonparticipation, opacity, and the undermining of autonomy highlight the importance of citizen participation in the creation, deployment, and redefinition of veils. But three important questions and issues remain:

i. What constitutes the appropriate kind of participation?
ii. When do citizens have the kind of access to veils that allows them to participate in this way?
iii. What kinds of steps can we take to promote this appropriate kind of participation?

Finding illuminating answers to these questions will require a close look at the complex dynamics involved in the creation, use, and altering of veils; I turn to this in section 4.3 and subsequent sections. However, we can see that the answer to (iii) will be linked to the ability of citizens to get information about the workings of their government.

The first, most natural, place to look is in the basic structure of the state and the rights that are formally extended to citizens. The process of creating and using veils falls within the broad category of political expression, so one indication of the level of participation possible in this respect is the level of protections given to that more general kind of expression. In the United States, for example, the Bill of Rights (and the First Amendment in particular) grants robust freedoms, such as freedom of speech and association, to individuals and groups. Other legislative measures (such as the Freedom of Information Act) give citizens wide access to information that the government uses in decision making. Similar constitutional provisions – either written or as part of an unwritten constitutional system – allowing citizens' freedom of speech and expression and access to government information can be found in almost all liberal democratic nations.

Formal institutions such as these protections and guarantees, however, can do only part of the work in allowing for participation with respect to veils. The needed supplement to formal measures is an active fostering of awareness of the uses of veils and the possibilities for private citizens to influence the content and application of political veils. A vibrant press and other dedicated watchdog groups and civil societies are all important for guarding against both a state monopoly over the production and use of veils and an overly trusting or naïve attitude toward those veils. Educational institutions – from primary schools to universities – are also important not just for disseminating information, but, more importantly, for enabling new generations of citizens to participate in the production of veils.

This still doesn't provide much insight into what citizen participation in the use and production of veils really means or amounts to, nor does it adequately express what this kind of participation is capable of doing. To give a better understanding of this, we need to consider a particular example of veils being created, used, and redefined over time by both political elites and the literally disenfranchised.

4.3. A STATE IN SEARCH OF A NATION

The case study I consider in this section is the role of the Declaration of Independence as a political veil that over time has had its meaning and significance stretched and reshaped in various ways by very different groups. The groups on which I focus are political elites (particularly, Jefferson and Lincoln) and African Americans, each of whom helped to define the present meaning of this political document in ways that nicely illustrate what participation means in this context. In particular, examining the effects of these quite conscious efforts to alter the meaning of the Declaration contrast with other, unintentional changes in the way this document was perceived.

But why focus on the Declaration, and why consider the impact of these particular groups? The significance of Jefferson is clear, since he was the author of the Declaration and most responsible for the rhetorical features of the document.[19] Lincoln is significant in his adept retelling of history that helped to cement in the popular imagination the priority of the Declaration over the Constitution.[20]

As two of the civic heroes of the United States, Jefferson and Lincoln might at least be expected to have the potential to shape and redefine the popular conception of the Declaration. What is more surprising is the extent to which some of the *least* powerful in the population – African Americans at a time when they were not just discriminated against,

---

[19] As the history of the Declaration is laid out in Joseph J. Ellis's *American Sphinx: The Character of Thomas Jefferson* (New York: Vintage Books, 1996, pp. 57–9), the committee charged with writing the Declaration consisted of Jefferson, John Adams, Benjamin Franklin, Robert Livingston, and Roger Sherman. The drafting took a few days, and Adams and Franklin made a few minor revisions before putting the Declaration to the Continental Congress, where it was approved on July 2, 1776.

[20] I have alluded to part of this story already at the beginning of Chapter 1.

but disenfranchised by law – had on the perceived significance of the Declaration. This, in turn, can be seen as having an important effect on perceptions toward what is owed to African Americans and what the promise of America's founding demanded.

4.3.1. Jefferson and the Design of a Veil

> *But what do we mean by the American Revolution? Do we mean the American war? The Revolution was effected before the war commenced. The Revolution was in the minds and hearts of the people; a change in their religious sentiments, of their duties and obligations.... This radical change in the principles, opinions, sentiments, and affections of the people was the real American Revolution.*
>
> John Adams to Hezekiah Niles, 1818[21]

The first and justly famous portion of the Declaration is a stirring manifesto:

When in the Course of human events, it becomes necessary for one people to dissolve the political bands which have connected them with another, and to assume among the Powers of the Earth, the separate and equal station to which the Laws of Nature and of Nature's God entitle them, a decent respect to the opinions of mankind requires that they should declare the causes which impel them to the separation.

We hold these truths to be self-evident, that all men are created equal, that they are endowed by their Creator with certain unalienable Rights, that among these are Life, Liberty, and the Pursuit of Happiness. That to secure these rights, Governments are instituted among Men, deriving their just powers from the consent of the governed, that whenever any Form of Government becomes destructive of these ends, it is the Right of the People to alter or abolish it....

This is, to be sure, powerful rhetoric. But if we are looking beyond the rhetorical power of Jefferson's language for a reason in the text for the central place the Declaration occupies, I think we are bound to be disappointed. A cynic might note that it is convenient that these truths are self-evident, for there is certainly no argument given *here* for them, nor any marshalling of evidence for these claims. That men are created equal with particular rights is hardly trivial, yet here we learn not just that, but

---

[21] Quoted in Bernard Bailyn, *Ideological Origins of the American Revolution* (Cambridge, MA: Harvard University Press, 1967), p. 160.

that the unalienable nature of those rights granted instant legitimacy to those who would resist regimes that didn't respect them – conveniently enough for American revolutionaries.

The rest of the Declaration *does* provide reasons to justify rebellion, but to modern ears many of those charges seem to be hyperbolic eighteenth century political "spin": The colonists are long-suffering and patient, and only reluctantly have been provoked by the excesses of King George III's tyranny. Given this language, it isn't hard to see how later historians would come to view the fears of the sort voiced by Jefferson in the Declaration as a mere propaganda ploy.[22]

Yet, if these fears are exaggerated (as they almost undoubtedly were), neither were they fabricated for purposes of manipulation. Instead, there is every reason to think they were an expression of Jefferson's sincere beliefs – ones that he shared with many leaders of the Revolution – and were of a piece with a long tradition in opposition literature in Britain. This tradition dated from the English Civil War in the mid-seventeenth century, and found its most influential expression in the work of "Country Party" writers John Trenchard, Thomas Gordon, Henry St. John Bolingbroke, and James Burgh.[23]

Jefferson himself was highly influenced by the hyperbolic and polemical style and ideology of these dissenters.[24] That helps to explain *his* rhetorical excesses. But more importantly, this sincere conviction that they were the victims of a massive conspiracy was quite common among Revolutionary leaders. As noted by the eminent historian Bernard Bailyn:

[T]he conviction on the part of the Revolutionary leaders that they were faced with a deliberate conspiracy to destroy the balance of the constitution and eliminate their freedom had deep and widespread roots – roots elaborately embedded

---

[22] Bailyn, ibid., pp. 157–8. See also Philip Davidson, *Propaganda and the American Revolution, 1763–1783* (Chapel Hill, NC: University of North Carolina Press, 1941); John C. Miller, *Sam Adams, Pioneer in Propaganda* (Stanford, CA: Stanford University Press, 1960).

[23] Bailyn, ibid., p. 35; Ellis, ibid., p. 49.

[24] Ellis, ibid. This influence, evident in the language of the Declaration, is particularly in Jefferson's *Declaration of the Causes and Necessities for Taking Up Arms*, in which he represents England as essentially ignoring the colonies until 1763, at which point the King turned toward oppressing Britain's faithful friends across the Atlantic. Ellis (ibid, p. 48) quotes a delegate from New York, William Livingston, as saying of this work: "Much fault-finding and declamation, with little sense of dignity. They seem to think a reiteration of tyranny, despotism, bloody, *etc.*, all that is needed to unite us at home."

in Anglo-American political culture. How far back in time one may trace these roots it is difficult to say, but ... the configuration of attitudes and ideas that would constitute the Revolutionary ideology was present a half-century before there was an actual Revolution. . . . [25]

In this context, it is natural to expect Jefferson's rhetoric in the Declaration to find a receptive audience. It employed a familiar literary style and voice, and dealt with the familiar theme of corrupt authority. Equally important was the fact that the standard it held up for legitimate government – the consistency of positive law and natural and inalienable rights – was itself the product of an argument that had raged for a century before the Revolution. In an important sense, then, the Declaration of Independence was a summary of the Revolutionary attitude and outlook, one that owed its power not to the novelty of its ideas, but to the fact that its principles and reasons were *not* novel – its ideas had, as suggested by the quotation from John Adams at the beginning of this section, been internalized by politically active colonists long before Jefferson put pen to paper. As noted by Carl Becker in his study of the Declaration, "Where Jefferson got his ideas is hardly so much a question as where he could have got away from them."[26]

This outlook was naturally propagated by the history written by Americans following the war. Through works like Mercy Otis Warren's *History of the American Revolution* and Jonathan Boucher's *View of the Causes and Consequences of the American Revolution*, the sincere conviction that the Revolution was sparked by a British conspiracy was transformed into a historical fact, and formed an essential part of a coherent story of beginnings. Of these histories, Bailyn observes that:

These are the histories of participants, or near-participants: heroic histories, highly personified and highly moral, in which the conspiratorial arguments propounded during the Revolution are the essential stuff of explanation. These views, caricatured and mythologized in such immortal potboilers as Weems'

---

[25] Bailyn, ibid., p. 144. Reflecting on the evolution of his own thoughts on the nature of Revolutionary rhetoric, Bailyn reports his own conclusion:

[T]here were real fears, real anxieties, a sense of real danger behind these phrases, and not merely the desire to influence by rhetoric and propaganda the inert minds of an otherwise passive populace. The more I read, the less useful, it seemed to me, was the whole idea of propaganda in its modern meaning when applied to the writings of the American Revolution (ibid., p. ix).

[26] Carl L. Becker, *The Declaration of Independence: A Study in the History of Political Ideas* (New York: Vintage, 1922), p. 27; see also pp. 25–6.

Washington, survived almost unaltered through the next generation – survived, indeed, through the next two generations – to enter in a new guise into the assumptions of twentieth-century scholarship.[27]

Note that this sketch of the origins and early history of the Declaration dovetails quite nicely with what we would expect in the creation of an effective political veil.[28] First, the style of the document was a familiar one to contemporary readers and the content – the themes and complaints Jefferson sounded in the Declaration – was, at least in the context of Revolutionary leaders, largely uncontroversial. As such, the superficial, stylistic aspects of the Declaration were both aesthetically appealing and familiar, while at the same time the substantive claims were ones that were already part of the political character of American leadership. Jefferson didn't have to convince his audience that the rights of life, liberty, and the pursuit of happiness were natural, nor that these rights would justify rebellion against corrupt British rule; it was enough that he distill the conclusions of a long, complex debate over the status of rights, legitimate government, representation, and consent into a single document that cut through these subtleties and highlighted what the leadership sincerely believed to be the essential issues of the American Revolution.

Second, the form of the histories that contributed to entrenching this view of the origins of the United States is noteworthy. These were not "disinterested" histories but heroic ones – "highly personified and highly moral" – and, as reported by Bailyn, the story they told was one that easily passed into a civic mythology surrounding both the Revolutionary generation and their circumstances. This, too, is what we might expect from a highly effective veil. And at the same time it helps to illuminate my claim in section 1.3 that the full weight of political veils can be appreciated only by considering how they are mutually supporting. We can see this facet of veils in the content of the history written in the wake of the Declaration and the Revolution. As indicated in the preceding quotation from Bailyn, representations of the Revolution assumed this perspective; it was something to be taken for granted in the analysis and explanation of events.

The central place of the Declaration in the popular image of America is testimony in part to these two factors. But even this much fails to account

---

[27] Bailyn, ibid., p. 157.
[28] See, in particular, sections 1.2 and 3.3.

for two popular conceptions: (i) that the Declaration is the founding document of the United States and (ii) that equality is a central value of the United States. To explain those conceptions, we need to turn to a process of redefinition of this veil in the period following the Revolution and culminating in Lincoln's Address at Gettysburg.

4.3.2. Lincoln: Redefining a Political Veil

Perhaps more than any other document of American politics, the Declaration has captured the imagination of citizens – both of the United States and of other countries. Ask the person on the street – in the United States or elsewhere – for the best and clearest statement of the founding principles of the United States and she is likely to point not to the Articles of Confederation, which were the first governing framework, nor even the Constitution or Bill of Rights. Rather, she is likely to name the Declaration of Independence, a document with no legally binding nature, one that has no formal standing as a constraint on either laws or institutions or practices public or private.

The first puzzle, then, concerns how the Declaration came to qualify as the "origin" of the United States. Taking the text literally, after all, suggests that the Declaration is more an ending than a beginning: It recounts reasons for dissolving the states's political connections to Great Britain, but hardly gives us a clue as to what the *new* government would be like.

The second puzzle concerns an interesting development in the relative importance of different parts of the Declaration. That is, the popular image of the Declaration not only represents it as the founding document of the United States, but as one that makes equality its central political and social value. On the face of it, this seems surprising, since the claim that "all men are equal" is but one of several "self-evident" truths claimed in the Declaration, including:

- All men are granted inalienable rights to life, liberty, and the pursuit of happiness.
- Governments derive their "just powers" from the consent of the governed.
- When a government is "destructive of these ends," the people have a right to replace it with one that "as to them shall seem most likely to effect their Safety and Happiness."

In its historical context, it is all the more surprising to find the Declaration being read as championing equality when many of the signers of the Declaration (including the author) were slave-holders. Further, if the commitment to equality *were* of such great importance to the Founders, we might reasonably expect this to turn up in other documents such as the Constitution. Yet there is *no* such reference in the Constitution, nor is this commitment part of the argument for ratification of the Constitution found in the *Federalist Papers*.[29]

What we find, then, is a shift in the way Americans perceived both the Declaration and the origins of the union. The major cause of this shift was Lincoln's Address at Gettysburg. With words that are nearly as famous as those of the Declaration itself, Lincoln brilliantly fixed the Declaration as the origin of the nation while at the same time identifying the aim to which that nation aspires:

Four score and seven years ago our fathers brought forth on this continent, a new nation, conceived in liberty, and dedicated to the proposition that all men are created equal.

The impact of the Address is hard to understate. As George Fletcher has argued in *Our Secret Constitution*, the Gettysburg Address created a new constitutional order for the United States. According to his arguments, the *original* Constitution of 1787 was based on the principle of personhood as a voluntary association with an exclusion of many other persons. Not so for the new principles that derive from the Address, which are directed at securing the equality of all persons.[30]

In his *Lincoln at Gettysburg*, Garry Wills makes clear that this was Lincoln's intention:

Both North and South strove to win the battle for *interpreting* Gettysburg as soon as the physical battle had ended. Lincoln is after even larger game – he means to "win" the whole Civil War in ideological terms as well as military ones. And he will succeed: the Civil War *is*, to most Americans, what Lincoln wanted it to *mean*. Words had to complete the work of the guns.[31]

[29] References to "equality" in *The Federalist Papers* are almost all ones that concern equality of states or nations.
[30] See Kendall and Carey, ibid., pp. 94–5, 138. See also Jeffrey Hart's introduction to Willmoore Kendall, *Willmoore Kendall Contra Mundum*, ed. Nellie D. Kendall (New Rochelle, NY: Arlington House, 1971), p. 20.
[31] Garry Wills, *Lincoln at Gettysburg: The Words That Remade America* (New York: Simon and Schuster, 1992), p. 38.

If the claim that Lincoln dramatically changed the way Americans thought – and continue to think – about themselves is surprising, it is only because of the success of his efforts. The shift is invisible to modern sensibilities: What could be more natural than to take the Declaration's assertion that "All men are created equal" for precisely what it says? Indeed, what else *could* it mean?

All this lends an aura of inevitability to the way we read the Declaration today. Yet, as noted previously, there are at least plausible reasons to think it was originally seen in a very different light, and it was Lincoln who was responsible for this change.

What he did was to redefine the meaning of a political veil. The Declaration of Independence was a symbol held in common by both North and South, by unionists and secessionists alike. The way he did this gives us a further illustration of how veils can be used and manipulated in a way that is quite consistent with liberal principles.

Like Jefferson, Lincoln didn't present a novel vision, but rather built on a doctrine that was devised by James Wilson in 1790, then developed in various ways through the first half of the nineteenth century. Within official governmental institutions, this doctrine was articulated by Henry Clay, Justice Joseph Story, and Daniel Webster; outside of government channels, it was voiced by abolitionists like Frederick Douglass and advocates of women's suffrage.[32] Lincoln didn't present the *argument* at Gettysburg, but instead presented an *image* – a *picture* for the public of the beginnings and purposes of a nation that encapsulated the conclusions of the argument in abstract, yet highly emotional, language:

> His speech is economical, taut, interconnected, like the machinery he tested and developed for battle. Words were weapons, for him, even though he meant them to be weapons of peace in the midst of war.
> This was the perfect medium for changing the way most Americans thought about the nation's founding acts. Lincoln does not argue law or history. . . . He *makes* history. He does not come to present a theory, but to impose a symbol, one tested in experience and appealing to natural values, with an emotional urgency entirely expressed in calm abstractions (fire in ice).[33]

By striking a variety of deeply engrained themes – Biblical motifs of covenant and renewal, the imagery of birth and death and rebirth, the

---

[32] See Wills, ibid, Chapter 4 for further discussion of the constitutional and legal foundation for Lincoln's assertion regarding the priority of the Declaration and the paramount value of equality.

[33] Ibid., p. 174.

classical model of funeral oratory – Lincoln drew upon a vast repository of feelings and emotions that he could channel for his purposes.[34] In so doing, he, like Jefferson did in crafting the Declaration itself, artfully used the tradition to change that tradition:

... He would cleanse the Constitution – not, as William Lloyd Garrison had, by burning an instrument that countenanced slavery. He altered the document from within, by appeal from its letter to the spirit, subtly changing the recalcitrant stuff of that legal compromise, bringing it to its own indictment.[35]

At the same time, by making his case rhetorically, Lincoln deftly deflected attempts to criticize his vision. One such attempt, articulated by conservative political theorists Willmoore Kendall and George Carey in their book *The Basic Symbols of the American Political Tradition*, contrasts the tradition of equalizing the social, economic, and political status of citizens established by Lincoln with an older tradition of self-government that affirms the equality of citizens only in a political sense. Like the editors of the *Chicago Times* immediately after the Address, advocates of this view see the equality tradition as a "derailment" – a betrayal – of the original American political tradition.

Conservative critics such as Kendall and Carey make a powerful argument for their view of America's origins. But this kind of criticism will strike many modern readers as ineffectual. The reason, I claim, is that Lincoln *didn't* engage the issue on the field of rational debate at Gettysburg. Instead, he attacked indirectly, using the rhetoric of the Address to impress a particular reading of history on the public:

In the crucible of the occasion, Lincoln distilled the meaning of the war, of the nation's purpose, of the remaining task, in a statement that is straightforward yet magical. No wonder the *Chicago Times* chafed impatiently at the Gettysburg Address. *Lincoln argues, but he also casts a spell; and what can a rebuttal do to incantation?*[36]

The way Lincoln moved people was *not* by argument or logic – although an argument *does* lie beneath the veil of rhetoric for those who will look. To respond to that rhetoric with an argument would be like responding to a poem with a legal brief or statistical table.[37] To cite law

[34] Ibid., pp. 88–9.
[35] Ibid., pp. 37–8.
[36] Ibid., pp. 88–9; emphasis added.
[37] Political rhetoric and slogans are particularly striking in their immunity to rational criticism. For instance, in the 1964 presidential election, the Goldwater campaign's

and history in response to the "spell" that Lincoln cast, then, is to miss Lincoln altogether. And, once the spell was cast, what Kendall and Carey called "Lincoln's heresy" – his attempt "to wrench from [the Declaration] a single proposition and make that our supreme commitment" – became the new orthodoxy.[38] In effect, "Lincoln's heresy" neatly erased from the American consciousness eighty years of controversy and contention over the meaning of the Declaration. Today, it seems to be simply taken for granted that there is no alternative to Lincoln's view.

There *has* been resistance to this view by intelligent, resourceful, and creative thinkers. Yet this resistance, no matter how carefully crafted or well supported, strikes many as impotent. Like philosophical arguments for solipsism or radical skepticism, they are intellectual curiosities, but nothing that alters the way we live. As Wills observed:

> For most people now, the Declaration means what Lincoln told us it means, as a way of correcting the Constitution itself without overthrowing it. It is this correction of the spirit, this intellectual revolution, that makes attempts to go back beyond Lincoln to some earlier version so feckless. *The proponents of states' rights may have arguments, but they have lost their force, in courts as well as in the popular mind. By accepting the Gettysburg Address, its concept of a single people dedicated to a proposition, we have been changed. Because of it, we live in a different America.*[39]

Lincoln's vision of America's origins remains – *not* because it won the debate with alternative visions on dispassionate, rational grounds, but because it changed *us* into a people that simply will not be moved by counterarguments.

4.3.3. Race, Equality, and the Declaration

My discussion so far has centered on the way that political elites have defined, used, and transformed the Declaration of Independence. In participatory regimes, however, influence on veils is not limited to elites. In this section, I explore some of the ways in which those who are *not* in a position of power – specifically, African Americans – have, like the

slogan was "In Your Heart You Know He's Right." How could the campaign have responded to the more memorable Democratic version of that slogan, "In Your Guts You Know He's Nuts"?

[38] Kendall and Carey, ibid., p. 91.

[39] Wills, ibid., pp. 146–7; emphasis added.

political elite, influenced the meaning we attribute to the Declaration of Independence.

On July 5, 1852, Frederick Douglass delivered a speech in Rochester, New York, entitled "The Meaning of July Fourth for a Negro":

What to the American slave is your 4th of July? I answer: a day that reveals to him, more than all other days in the year, the gross injustice and cruelty to which he is the constant victim. . . . To him, . . . your shouts of liberty and equality, a hollow mockery; your prayers and hymns, your sermons and thanksgivings, with all your religious parade and solemnity, are, to him, mere bombast, fraud, deception, impiety, and hypocrisy – *a thin veil to cover up crimes which would disgrace a nation of savages* . . .[40]

Here we find Douglass arguing (as Lincoln would eleven years later) from both the primacy of the Declaration and a reading of that document as making equality the paramount virtue of the United States. But could Douglass seriously have believed the founders – many of whom (including Jefferson) owned slaves – actually intended it to have applied to slaves?

It would be ridiculous to claim that Douglass somehow failed to appreciate the gap between reality and what he was claiming the Declaration promised. But what, then, could he have been up to in making this claim? The philosopher Charles Mills suggests that Douglass was acting in "bad faith." That is, if we read Douglass as offering up an *argument* for equality, his reading of the Declaration constitutes a *premise*. Since that reading in no way corresponded to the popular image of the Declaration, Douglass was either a fool or a charlatan to cite it as a premise.[41]

Yet this seems rather uncharitable to Douglass – and further, his reasoning would have startling implications for our assessment of *other* political rhetoric. By thinking in terms of veils and their manipulation, we have what I think is a better reading of Douglass's purposes. Just as Wills said of Lincoln, Douglass should not be thought of as "arguing law or history," but as *making* history by putting the Declaration of Independence to use as a political tool to change the condition of African

---

[40] Frederick Douglass, "The Meaning of July Fourth for a Negro," in Philip S. Foner, ed., *The Life and Writings of Frederick Douglass*, Vol. 2, *Pre-Civil War Decades, 1850–1860* (New York: International Publishers Co., 1950).

[41] For more on social criticism, see Michael Walzer, *Interpretation and Social Criticism* (Cambridge, MA: Harvard University Press, 1987); *The Company of Critics* (New York: Basic Books, 1988).

Americans. To do this, he quite sensibly appealed to a powerful veil, framing it in a way that highlighted a prima facie conflict between its text (however that text really *ought* to be interpreted) and reality.

The case of Douglass illustrates how the use of political veils in a participatory regime is available to even oppressed groups. That is, even given the limitations on what he, a former slave in the 1850s, could do, Douglass was committed to using existing traditions and institutions as the means of changing them.[42] In Douglass we also see an interesting case of appropriation of a symbol for the purpose of liberalization.

As I have argued previously, the legitimate use of veils demands (among other things) that the symbols, myths, and traditions be a people's own. It is the "ownership" of symbols that provides the motivational force of veils. As such, we might expect the Declaration to "connect with" those free white Americans who were the direct heirs to the arguments and doctrines that arose in the decades before the Revolution.

What may seem more surprising, however, is that the slave population – presumably cut off from pre-Revolutionary political and social developments – should be moved by the Declaration as well. Yet a closer look at the traditions to which African Americans were heirs helps to resolve this puzzle just as we would expect on my account of veil politics.

The puzzle concerns why African Americans so enthusiastically appropriated the symbol of the Declaration – particularly its assertion regarding equality. As it turns out, many West African cultures (from where many slaves hailed) share a tradition of regarding all human beings equal with respect to their having an essential element, one that the Akan of Ghana called *Okra*, the "spark" of the Supreme Being. By virtue of having this spark of the Supreme Being, all human beings are entitled to basic human dignity, responsibilities, and rights.[43]

---

[42] Indeed, Douglass's break with the abolitionist William Lloyd Garrison was a result of their differing views on the possibility of using the Constitution as a means of ending slavery.

[43] The expression "spark of the Supreme Being" here is more accurately interpreted as referring to the primitive sense of value accorded to the individual than something like the Christian notion of a soul. Note also that the term *human being* has a meaning distinct from that of the term *person*. In the West African understanding, one is either a human being or one is not; there is no such thing as *becoming* a human being. It is, however, possible for someone to become a *person*, and in most of Africa, the concept of personhood admits of gradation: The higher the achievement, the more of a person one becomes. For a detailed treatment of this topic, see Kwasi Weridu, *Cultural Universals and Particulars* (Bloomington,

The belief that all human being deserve the same consideration and rights, then, had deeps roots in the traditions shared by many enslaved Africans. And, just as immigrants to America brought their own religious, social, and political traditions with them to the New World, so too did enslaved Africans. Thus, while European and West African cultures differ in many deep and fundamental ways, they share enough to allow members of each to respond to claims to "self-evident" truth about the equality of all persons.[44]

The course of the civil rights movement provides additional examples of how oppressed people can use veils for liberalization and empowerment. In his "Letter from Birmingham Jail," for instance, Martin Luther King, Jr., appeals to traditions shared by the vast majority of Americans. Biblical rhetoric and imagery pervade the letter; responding to the charge that he is an unwanted outside stirring up trouble, he argued that he not only had long-standing links to the Birmingham community, but was invited; like St. Paul, he "must constantly respond to the Macedonian call for aid."[45]

The political tradition to which he appeals is one in which Lincoln and Jefferson march arm in arm as fellow radicals with a simple, straightforward message of equality. King eloquently argued from that tradition with a direct appeal to what by 1963 was the new orthodoxy – Lincoln's orthodoxy – regarding the Declaration and its promise:

When the architects of *our* republic wrote the magnificent words of the Constitution and the Declaration of Independence, they were signing a promissory note to which *every American* was to fall heir. This note was a promise that *all* men would be guaranteed the inalienable rights of life, liberty, the pursuit of happiness.

I have a dream that one day this nation will rise up and live out the true meaning of its creed: "We hold these truths to be self-evident: that all men are created equal."

I have a dream that one day ... *little black boys and black girls will be able to join hands with little white boys and white girls and walk together as sisters and brothers.*

IN: Indiana University Press, 1996), Chapter 8; and Kwame Gyekye, *An Essay on African Philosophical Thought* (Philadelphia, PA: Temple University Press, 1978), Chapter 2.

44 Part of the powerful attraction of Christianity to African Americans is undoubtedly due to the faith's content. But it may be equally significant that at least some African cultures share a deep metaphysical commitment similar to that of Christianity.

45 S. Jonathan Bass, *Blessed Are the Peacemakers: Martin Luther King, Jr., Eight White Religious Leaders, and the "Letter from Birmingham Jail"* (Baton Rouge, LA: LSU Press, 2001), p. 239.

Here, too, the King speech was inclusive. In no small part this was because of his use of references and phrases – the Constitution, the Declaration of Independence, "our republic," "every American" – that left no Americans in the cold. He knew that "freedom" was sacred to the United States and so appealed to freedom:

> So let freedom ring from the prodigious hilltops of New Hampshire. Let freedom ring from the mighty mountains of New York. Let freedom ring from the heightening Alleghenies of Pennsylvania! Let freedom ring from snowcapped Rockies of Colorado! Let freedom ring from the curvaceous peaks of California!

With the precision, beauty, and richness of poetry and the clarity of prose, he juxtaposed the "self-evident truth" against the harsh reality of racism. Like Lincoln at Gettysburg, King's greatness was not in the novelty of his ideas, but in his careful and effective use of what came before him in the public imagination. His narrative was built on the narratives of Lincoln, the founding fathers, and ultimately on the shared Judeo-Christian and African rock-bottom custom of basic equal humanity and dignity. By placing these narratives at the base and honoring his political ancestors, he then brought in his own narratives to solve the problems of his day.

4.4. CONCLUSION

> *Circus dogs jump when the trainer cracks his whip, but the really well-trained dog is the one that turns the somersault when there is no whip.*
>
> – George Orwell[46]

One of the fundamental aims of a liberal state is to support the autonomy of its citizens by helping to empower citizens to control their own lives. One threat to autonomy, of course, is the existence of blatant and oppressive constraints that openly deny citizens this kind of self-control. What our examination of political veils suggests, however, is that there is a more insidious threat to autonomy. As part of the backdrop to everyday life, veils have the capacity to bias choices in dramatic ways, supporting particular values and practices over others, and in so doing, inclining citizens toward certain kinds of actions or (more plausibly) making certain options "invisible" to citizens. Under the spell cast by potent veils,

---

[46] George Orwell, "As I Please," *Tribune*, July 7, 1944. Quoted in Michael Shelden, *Orwell* (New York: HarperCollins, 1990), p. 367.

it may be that citizens don't reject alternative policies and practices as much as they fail to see those policies and practices as alternatives at all. Like Orwell's "really well-trained dog," citizens in this case will turn their "somersaults" both dutifully and without prompting.

To check threats to autonomy, we can insist that regimes be participatory: The power of these states derives from the consent of the governed, and through representation, citizens have a voice in the laws that govern them. Participation of this sort is commonly taken to amount to formal measures, such as universal suffrage, equal protection under the law, and free and open elections. To limit our concern to these formal measures, however, is to overlook the significant effect of informal factors – the significance of veils. Just as important is the ability of citizens of various political, social, and economic classes to use and alter veils for political purposes. This ability empowers citizens to make changes not just to the *letter* of the law, but to the very *character* of the population that, far more than the written law, affects the lives of individuals.

There are, of course, important connections between formal and informal measures concerning participation. Freedom of speech and the press, for instance, is an important condition for citizens to influence how others view particular symbols or historical figures. But while certain formal measures may be necessary for citizens to be able to participate in the crafting of veils, there is no good reason to think that they are sufficient. As I have argued in section 4.1, manipulative, purely mythic, and colonized regimes may well fail to allow this kind of participation in a number of ways – despite having all the formal accoutrement of a liberal polity. The result is a state that either reneges on the promise of a genuine participation or reduces to a formal political structure that cannot engage with the public.

Genuinely participatory regimes are ones in which citizens not only have the formal means of participating in the governing process, but can create and control the meanings of veils in various ways as well. As illustrated by Jefferson's creation of the Declaration of Independence or Lincoln's "heresy," this control may be dramatic and intentional, coming from the very top of the political structure. In other cases, changes may be more gradual, with private citizens in different positions of power helping to reshape political veils. With respect to participation in the creation and redefinition of veils, perhaps the most important and interesting cases to consider are those in which myths and symbols arise from the public at large. The example of the Vietnam War Memorial discussed in section 3.4.1 was the product of just such a "bottom-up" effort, and the examples of yellow ribbons that appeared during the Iranian hostage crisis of the late 1970s or the renewed symbolic meaning of the American flag following the terrorist attacks on September 11, 2001, are particularly striking illustrations of how uncoordinated, spontaneous action on the part of common citizens can produce and affect political veils.

In figures like Jefferson, Lincoln, Douglass, and King, we find individuals particularly gifted in appealing to these veils; they are, I would claim, consummate practitioners of veil politics. But this skill should be carefully distinguished from mere silver-tongued demagoguery or rhetorical manipulation of the public. Each took an *existing* tradition and applied it to a particular political purpose, tapping into deep emotions and using them as an engine to drive political change.[47]

The difference between participatory and nonparticipatory regimes, then, is not just a matter of the laws on the books – although these formal features are certainly important. Rather, the essential difference turns on the actual degree of control that citizens have over their government. All the formal protections in the world will not protect citizens who, either through outright manipulation by elites, lack of imagination, or lack of familiarity, are powerless to alter the playing field on which those formal protections are deployed and arguments over their precise meanings and implications are conducted.

---

[47] This should in no way, however, be mistaken for their rejecting the value and function of rational debate. As I have argued in section 3.4, one of the conditions of a liberal veil includes its justification to the population – either actually or (more commonly) hypothetically. This requires that there be something more to the veil than its superficial features; ideally, the superficial features should be no more compelling to the casual onlooker than the deep nature of the veiled object should be to the well-informed rational deliberator. Each figure considered in this chapter had arguments, reasons, and principles that served as a theoretical basis for his or her positions; as such, the appeals to symbols and traditions satisfy a necessary condition for liberal veils.

Chapter 5

Civic Education in a Liberal State

> [I]n all political societies which have had a durable existence,
> there has been some fixed point; something which men agreed
> in holding sacred; which . . . was in common estimation placed
> beyond discussion.
>
> – John Stuart Mill[1]

Just as delicate plants that thrive in one climate may wither in another, political structures and institutions that are stable and engage citizens in *one* set of circumstances may be highly unstable and fail to engage citizens in *another* situation. To spread liberal democracy to the developing world (and support it where it already exists), it is crucial to identify the conditions that influence the fortunes of liberalism in particular situations.

Liberal theorists have generally acknowledged that certain material factors are necessary for liberalism to be a viable political system.[2] More interesting (and controversial) is the need for a common set of values, beliefs, or practices – Mill's "fixed points" or core civic commitments. One of these values is autonomy, or the capacity of individuals to make their own choices by reflecting rationally and deliberately on the alternatives.[3] Another of these core values is that of tolerance for other ways of life.

---

[1] John Stuart Mill, *Mill on Bentham and Coleridge* (Westport, CT: Greenwood Press, 1950), p. 123.
[2] In *A Theory of Justice*, for instance, Rawls confines himself to situations in which citizens are not so badly off that they are preoccupied with survival.
[3] See section 3.1 for my discussion of the nature of autonomy and the relationship between autonomy and veils.

It is not hard to see how these two values may conflict. On the one hand, allowing custom, tradition, or habit to have undue influence over a person's course in life means those choices would not be hers in the way required for autonomy. Promoting autonomy by promoting rational deliberation may seem at first to be precisely the kind of neutral stance that one would want in a polity dedicated to tolerance. Yet a moment's reflection will suggest otherwise, for diverse liberal states are almost certain to have significant groups of individuals whose moral or religious beliefs are incompatible with this "enlightened" method of deliberation.[4]

The main debate within liberal civic education concerns the question of what we ought to do with these citizens. How, that is, can we promote those civic values that each citizen of a liberal state should adopt – Mill's "fixed points" – to a degree sufficient to maintain a modern liberal state while at the same time respecting the special values of tolerance, equality, and liberty that are essential components of liberalism? Any attempt to balance these two values risks two undesirable consequences. The first is that in promoting the autonomy of citizens, we impose an unduly restrictive course of civic education on citizens. The second is that we err on the side of accommodating too many ways of life, and in the process fail to instill the kind of character needed for a thriving liberal democracy.

This is one instance of the perennial problem of political philosophy: determining the proper weighting of different values. And this problem of identifying the proper aims of civic education is the one that has drawn the most attention by theorists. Largely overlooked, however, are the difficulties that arise in realizing those aims. Existing accounts of civic education are, then, incomplete in a crucial respect, since they leave a gap between their vision of how a liberal state ought to be and the current state of affairs.

In this chapter, I shall argue that veil politics helps to span this gap between where we find ourselves and the far side we wish to reach.

---

[4] This is *not* to say that those who appeal to divine revelation or to tradition in making their judgments reject reason or the importance of rationality. For instance, if you ask a fundamentalist why she believes what she does, she will often be happy to give you her reasons for relying on, for example, some literal reading of a sacred text rather than some other source. It may be more accurate, then, to characterize fundamentalists and others who see their way of life threatened by rationalism not as rejecting reason altogether, but as rejecting a comprehensive rationalism that refuses to recognize their own sources as valid ones.

Methodologically, it points us to the materials we can use to build our "bridge" – to existing customs and traditions, to symbols and myths that already are connected to the character and judgments of citizens. Conceptually, it gives us a set of analytic tools appropriate for those materials, and provides a theoretical framework for thinking about how veils can be used in service of liberal aims.

5.1. MODELS OF LIBERAL CIVIC EDUCATION

Like any other kind of polity, a liberal state requires that its members share at least some values or virtues. These include those necessary to *any* polity (such as a sense of cohesion among citizens and loyalty to the state) as well as special liberal values, such as civic tolerance and respect for others and their conceptions of the good.

In recognition of this, advocates (*and* critics) of liberalism today typically acknowledge that *some* form of civic education is necessary for liberal democratic states.[5] An important tradition in liberal civic education is one that focuses on the rational capacities of citizens. It is hardly surprising that liberal approaches to civic education should be closely linked to reason, for if there is a theme to varieties of liberal political theories it is that reason is intimately bound together with "right conduct" (where this is understood in either a moral or political sense). This view of political education, then, is a natural development of modern liberalism's commitment to using reason to define and identify our moral and political obligations.[6]

Central to this program is the presumption that one key to getting citizens to recognize and act in accordance with their obligations as citizens is to help them develop their rational faculties. The intelligent, well-informed citizen, reasons the liberal civic pedagogue, is a virtuous citizen of a liberal state; therefore, teaching rational deliberation and tolerance for alternative ways of life is enough to motivate citizens to act as required for a thriving, well-functioning liberal state.

---

[5] For a representation of the major views and theorists in the field, see the "Symposium On Citizenship, Democracy, and Education," edited by Stephen Macedo and published in *Ethics* 105 (1995).

[6] The deontological tradition in liberal thought deriving from Kantian doctrine holds that insofar as we are rational agents, we *cannot* act contrary to those obligations. The consequentialist tradition assigns reason a similar role as the means by which individuals identify their civic obligations.

Proposals concerning liberal civic education are typically shaped by two of liberalism's basic values: individual autonomy and nonrepression. To uphold the former, liberal states are committed to helping citizens to control their own lives. Given the traditional (and entirely plausible) links between rationality and autonomy laid out in section 2.3, the commitment to promoting autonomy is usually seen in turn as a commitment to promoting the use of rational deliberation in citizens. Other things being equal, the state has a responsibility to get citizens to make their life choices by some kind of rational investigation – by weighing evidence and considering alternatives in an open-minded, critical, and unbiased way – rather than looking to tradition, custom, or religious revelation.

While committed to promoting autonomy in this way, however, the liberal state is also committed to nonrepression. If we consider states composed of individuals who are already rational, it isn't hard to see how this claim to nonrepression could be satisfied. In states such as these, one can hope to appeal to citizens' rational capacities in order to persuade rather than to force them to act in one way rather than another.

Unfortunately, the methods of education appropriate for these two goals of autonomy and nonrepression are not always so neatly aligned as we might hope. If we restrict our attention to citizens who are already rational in the required sense, of course, there is no tension between the two. But when we relax that restriction, we cannot simply assume that citizens will be moved by reason in this way. And relax this we must, for in the real world, not everyone wants to live the life of rational deliberation. For these individuals, imposing the kind of education required to make them rational amounts to the very kind of repression the liberal state aims to avoid.

Resolving the tension generated by the twin commitments to autonomy and nonrepression is a central problem of liberal civic education – so central that we can usefully divide approaches to liberal civic education according to the relative importance of these two aims.[7] Some

---

[7] As William Galston has observed in "Civic Education in the Liberal State" (in *Liberalism and the Moral Life*, ed. Nancy L. Rosenblum, Cambridge, MA: Harvard University Press, 1989, p. 95), the difficulty of balancing autonomy and nonrepression may be a problem unique to liberalism; unlike most other political structures, liberalism refuses to give politics primacy over all other kinds of associations (such as familial and religious ones). Ultimately, the tension I am highlighting may reduce (as do so many other particular issues related to liberalism) to the perennial debate within liberalism over the proper bounds of individual privacy.

will argue that training citizens to be critical, questioning deliberators is paramount, and that this objective trumps the claims of those who would prefer to live a less self-critical life.[8] If this kind of education should clash with some particular lifestyle – even one that was otherwise consistent with a liberal state – then that lifestyle must give way.

For others, this priority is reversed. While maintaining a commitment to autonomy and rationality, these individuals stress the importance of respecting as wide a range of individual conceptions of the good as possible. This position allows (among other things) parents to restrict exposure of their children to materials that may promote rational skills, but which conflict with or undermine other values cherished by the parents. Such a view does not hold that liberalism be neutral among *all* conceptions of the good. Rather, it maintains only that liberalism should be neutral between those conceptions of the good *with respect to their view of rationality*. The state may, for instance, restrict lifestyles that hold to divinely revealed racist behavior, but only because of the racist component, not because its source is revelation rather than reason.

This debate is one over the *aims* of civic education – a debate, as it were, over the features, contours, and qualities of the society we *hope* to make. This is, no doubt, part of developing a program of civic education. But if an account of civic education focuses exclusively on that feature, it will say nothing about the more practical issue of how, once these aims are identified, we are to achieve them. As I argue in this chapter, existing accounts of civic education are fundamentally incomplete in this way, and any realistic model of liberal civic education must be supplemented with an appeal to veils.

---

[8] I hasten to add that while I distinguish two approaches, the difference between them is one of emphasis, not that between far-flung extremes. In most particular situations, the two sides will agree on policy (albeit giving different reasons). When they differ, it is typically over cases that are from the outset regarded as highly controversial, and where there is a plausible case to be made for each. The ubiquitous references in the literature on liberal civic education to a handful of specific cases – *Yoder v. Wisconsin, Mozert v. Hawkins County Board of Education* – testify to the rather narrow (but theoretically significant) difference between the two perspectives. For further examples of controversial cases involving civic education, see Meira Levinson, *The Demands of Liberal Education* (Oxford, UK: Oxford University Press, 1999), especially Chapter 4, in which she compares civic education in three democratic countries: France, Britain, and the United States.

5.1.1. Education for Autonomy: Gutmann on Civic Education

One of the most influential discussions of civic education today is that of Amy Gutmann.[9, 10] On her account, the proper aim of civic education is to develop the ability of citizens to make their own choices. According to Gutmann, the two main conditions for this ability are rationality and tolerance. The former enables individuals effectively to pursue their own aims; the latter ensures that nothing unfairly biases the choices of those individuals (even if others *know* that they will regret those choices). The anticipated result of this education is the enhancement of individual autonomy. From a theoretical perspective, this fits autonomy and nonrepression together quite nicely, and make Gutmann's program of civic education very attractive.

This program is designed to instill in citizens a rational character; in so doing, its aim is to promote a *process* of deliberation rather than a particular set of choices. Ultimately, of course, the choices and actions of citizens are of great importance; those, after all, are what dictate the course of the state as a whole. But Gutmann's focus on process captures a general nonconsequentialist feature of liberal thought, that is, that while consequences are important, they cannot make us indifferent to the causal paths that lead to them.

A clear indication of the importance that Gutmann assigns to the process of decision making is the fact that she makes deliberation essential to the desired result of civic education, what she refers to as *conscious social*

---

9 My discussion of Gutmann draws primarily from her "Undemocratic Education," in *Liberalism and the Moral Life*, ed. Nancy L. Rosenblum (Cambridge, MA: Harvard University Press, 1989), pp. 71–88. See also her *Democratic Education* (Princeton, NJ: Princeton University Press, 1987); "Civic Education and Social Diversity," *Ethics* 105 (April 1995), pp. 55–79. For a similar account, see Eamonn Callan's "Tradition and Integrity in Moral Education," *American Journal of Education* 101 (November 1992), pp. 1–28, and "Political Liberalism and Political Education," *Review of Politics* 58 (Winter 1996), pp. 5–33.

10 Gutmann's is an explicitly democratic model of civic education, and she is well aware that there is an important conceptual difference between democracy and liberalism. In particular, she stresses the importance of democratic processes in decision making more than orthodox liberals, who would be inclined to make exceptions to democratic procedures if doing so were likely to further liberal aims. That said, however, she also acknowledges (*Democratic Education*, p. 9, n. 19) that there are natural ways in which liberal and democratic civic education proposals will converge, and hers is often cited as a model of liberal civic education. See, for instance, Emily R. Gill, *Becoming Free: Autonomy and Diversity in the Liberal Polity* (Lawrence, KS: University of Kansas Press, 2001).

reproduction. As conceived of by Gutmann, conscious social reproduction requires not just passing on of a code of conduct, but also involves instilling a particular kind of rational character intimately linked to the methods of inference and deliberation used by citizens.

At the very least, this renders illegitimate any efforts to inhibit rational discourse:

[F]or a society to reproduce itself consciously, it must be non-repressive. It must not restrict rational consideration of different ways of life.[11]

The requirements for conscious social reproduction go far beyond this, however, for as Gutmann makes clear, it not only prohibits constraints on rational deliberation, but obligates the state to encourage and foster deliberation of this sort:

[The state] must cultivate the kind of character and the kind of intellect that enable people to choose rationally (some would say "autonomously") among different ways of life.... Nonrepression is not a principle of purely negative freedom. It secures freedom from interference only to the extent that it forbids using education to restrict rational deliberation or consideration of different ways of life. Nonrepression is therefore compatible with – indeed it requires – the use of education to inculcate those character traits, such as honesty, religious toleration, and mutual respect for persons, that serve as foundations for rational deliberation of differing ways of life.[12]

Promoting the ability of individuals rationally to entertain alternatives and discriminate among them is one important component in allowing them to control their own lives. But this ability is meaningful only if there are options – live, realistic alternative ways of life – available. For that reason, Gutmann argues that the liberal state has a further obligation to foster an attitude of mutual respect in citizens regarding other ways of life, an attitude that she makes clear goes beyond mere tolerance:

A more distinctive democratic virtue that a good society must also teach is mutual respect for differences of opinion. Mutual respect demands more than the attitude of live and let live; it requires the willingness and ability to accord due intellectual and moral regard to reasonable points of view that we cannot ourselves accept as correct.[13]

[11] Gutmann, "Undemocratic Education," p. 77.
[12] Ibid., pp. 77–8.
[13] Ibid., p. 75.

112

The purpose of supporting this kind of mutual respect, Gutmann claims, is *not* to weaken the conviction that citizens have regarding the ways of life they have chosen for themselves: one can respect an opposing view while rejecting it as ill-founded or mistaken. Rather, it is to enhance the choice of new members for the state (primarily children growing into adulthood) by presenting them with a wide range of options, each of which is publicly acknowledged to be at least reasonable.

In these circumstances, parents with particular moral or religious convictions may encourage those same views in their children, and in the process criticize views that are incompatible with their own. What they *cannot* do – and what the state may legitimately intervene to stop – is, to close the minds of their children to those alternatives entirely. By promoting the reasonableness of these alternative views, the state ensures that children have meaningful choices when they decide on their path in life:

> A state makes choice possible by teaching future citizens respect for opposing points of view and ways of life. It makes choice meaningful by equipping children with the intellectual skills necessary to evaluate ways of life different from that of their parents.[14]

What to critics is a gratuitous intrusion into the rights of people to live unreflective, uncritical lives is, from Gutmann's perspective, an essential component in supporting every citizen's ability to make her own choices.

5.1.2. *The Problem of Implementation*

Gutmann is, I think, quite correct to claim that liberal democratic states are committed to supporting citizens' abilities to choose their own way of life. Indeed, her claims about the aims of civic education and the kind of character it is supposed to instill are, while controversial, ones that even critics should agree are plausible and well motivated.

Still, her account is incomplete in a crucial respect, for she fails to provide any details about how we are to realize these aims. In this sense, hers is representative of most other discussions of civic education in its focus on identifying the legitimate or justifiable ends of such education rather than on the more practical problem of achieving those ends. While

[14] Gutmann, *Democratic Education* (Princeton, NJ: Princeton University Press, 1987), p. 30.

this is part of what we need, it is only part; the mere fact that we have good reasons to *want* to do something in no way means that we *can* do it.

Despite the fact that Gutmann provides few explicit suggestions about how civic education should be delivered, we can still discern some general guidelines or constraints on the means that she would regard as appropriate. Most importantly, the fact that her account is aimed at supporting conscious social reproduction suggests that the process by which children develop the values and character of virtuous liberal citizens is itself one that must be conscious, rational, and deliberate. I refer to this kind of approach as *deliberative civic education*.

This deliberative approach dovetails nicely with the presumed aims of civic education, and flatters a powerful a priori intuition that causes must be similar to their effects. Just as we might reject spontaneous generation by claiming that life comes only from life, so too we might reject approaches to civic education that seize upon irrational (or *a*-rational factors) on the grounds that such an approach cannot "produce" rational and deliberation agents.

Gutmann herself seems to embrace this causal principle when she explicitly distinguishes *socializing* forces from *educational* forces. Of the former, she writes:

Most political scientists who write about education subsume it under the concept of political socialization. Political socialization is typically understood to include the processes by which democratic societies transmit political values, attitudes, and modes of behavior to citizens. Since many of these processes are unintended, political socialization studies tend to focus on what might be called "unconscious social reproduction."[15]

In acknowledging this unconscious process of socialization, Gutmann clearly recognizes that myriad factors – rhetoric, images, customs, and so on – play a role in shaping the character of future citizens. Yet she immediately sets consideration of these forces aside as irrelevant to *her* purposes as a democratic (and, presumably, liberal[16]) theorist:

The focus of political socialization studies makes sense as long as their aim is to *explain* the processes by which societies perpetuate themselves. If one's aim is instead to understand how members of a democratic society *should* participate

---

[15] Ibid., p. 15.
[16] See footnote 10.

in consciously shaping its future, then it is important not to assimilate education with political socialization.[17]

The character of citizens, then, depends not only on the *values* that our program of civic education promotes, but also on the *manner* in which those values are promoted.

Two questions arise from this position. The first concerns the *practicality* of her proposal: Is it realistic to think that rational appeals of this sort are sufficient to instill the desired values? The second concerns the *need* for the constraints she imposes on the implementation of civic education: Is there good reason to think the *only* way to produce self-conscious rational deliberators is to use a self-conscious, rational, and deliberative style of civic education? In other words, can her appeals to rationality really provide the basis for empathy among the citizenry, or the public spiritedness and patriotism essential to any state? Can they be counted on to instill particular liberal values such as tolerance for other ways of life or develop a commitment to the extent and limits of a liberal conception of individual liberty? And if they cannot, are there alternatives ways of instilling those same values?

To answer these questions, imagine civic education à la Gutmann, perhaps in the form of a class discussion of the legacy of slavery in which students debate various views. One hopes that this process will create in students a clear, deep, and abiding appreciation for the evils of slavery. More plausibly, however, the kind of genuinely open-minded discourse Gutmann seems to have in mind will have a rather different effect. Students would, of course, discuss the undeniable horrors and degradation suffered by slaves and the effects of slavery on their descendents. But they would *also* be presented with the possibility that descendents of slaves are better off for having been born in the United States rather than in Africa, along with views that deny that slavery has had a lingering legacy.[18] While the latter claims may be controversial, they fall well within the range of what a responsible, rational, and well-informed person could sincerely believe to be the truth.[19]

---

[17] Gutmann, *Democratic Education*, p. 15; emphasis added.
[18] A case is made for the first of these positions in Kenneth B. Richburg, *Out of America: A Black Man Confronts Africa* (New York: HarperCollins, 1997).
[19] My discussion of the Declaration of Independence in Chapter 4 provides another example of the difficulties implicit in using rational debate to generate widespread agreement among citizens (particularly with respect to issues of values and significance). There I discussed a view of the American political tradition that is in startling respects inconsistent with the "received view" today. Yet this reading is

The effect of this kind of process is almost inevitably a blurring of distinctions that at first blush seemed quite sharp. Subject a "simple and obvious truth" – "I have a body," "slavery is an unmitigated evil" – to some open-minded philosophical analysis, and a raft of complications and nuances is revealed. This is *not* to say that this kind of analysis inevitably overturns those prior judgments or leads to skepticism (and I certainly don't deny that I have a body or that slavery is an evil!). But if it doesn't necessarily lead one to *those* positions, neither does it necessarily lead to any *other* particular position – including the highly nontrivial and controversial position occupied by liberalism.[20]

In many situations, it is a virtue to be able to see the other side (or sides) of an argument, and to acknowledge the fallible nature of our beliefs. Any realistic appraisal of the nature of rationality (of the sort offered in section 2.3.1) will show that with respect to many issues, *rationality is equivocal*: Rational agents deliberating on the same information can (and often will) reach different conclusions.[21] Indeed, getting people to appreciate the equivocal nature of rationality seems as if it would be an important aim of a Gutmann-style approach to civic education, for a salient feature of a liberal character is the understanding that reasonable people may disagree even after all the information is in.

Yet there must be a limit to this as well. It is one thing to engage in a free-wheeling debate over fundamental civic values in a seminar, but quite another thing if these commitments are genuinely "up for grabs." In politics, at least, there are no "views from nowhere."[22] Any

---

hardly irrational. In fact, perhaps the best explanation for why so many today would find it objectionable is not that it was the loser in an open debate, but the mere fact that it rejects conclusions to which the vast majority of Americans are already committed.

[20] It is the equivocal nature of rationality to which Galston refers when he notes: "[T]he greatest threat to children in modern liberal societies is not that they will believe in something too deeply, but that they will believe in nothing very deeply at all. Even to achieve the kind of free self-reflection that many liberals prize, it is better to begin by believing something" ("Civic Education in the Liberal State," in *Education and the Moral Life*, ed. Rosenblum, p. 101).

[21] As Bas van Fraassen has noted in another context, the presumptive cornerstone of rationality, deductive logic, doesn't tell us what inferences are obligatory, but only those that are permissible. (Bas C. van Fraassen, *The Scientific Image* (Oxford, UK: Clarenden Press, 1980).

[22] I borrow this phrase from Thomas Nagel's *The View from Nowhere* (Oxford, UK: Oxford University Press, 1986). The phrase is used along the same lines by Eamonn Callan, in "Beyond Sentimental Education," *American Journal of Education* 102 (1994), p. 205.

stable kind of polity – liberal, democratic, or otherwise – demands a broad commitment among its citizens to *some* set of values or another, a commitment that is *not* provisional in the way that we might think belief in, say, a scientific theory should be.[23]

What, precisely, these commitments are will vary from state to state. No state, however, is neutral with respect to the values that its citizens hold; for each, there are positions that are simply beyond the pale, ones that are ruled out either by fiat or (more politely, perhaps) by claims that such positions are simply unreasonable.[24] The problem then concerns how rational discourse *by itself* will lead to this kind of commitment either to specifically liberal values or to the more general virtues of loyalty and law-abidingness that *any* state will require. If, as I have suggested, reason is equivocal with respect to these kinds of issues, we will have to look *beyond* reason to secure this kind of commitment.[25]

There is, in addition to the equivocal nature of reason, an even deeper problem with relying solely on deliberative civic education. The preceding problem grants that the subjects of civic education are capable of this kind of deliberation. This, however, already assumes a great deal, for the skills and sensibilities that this process requires are hardly trivial. Those who are unmoved by your best arguments but unable to present a compelling objection or alternative may simply be stubbornly refusing

---

[23] It is worth noting that not even scientific commitments may be provisional in this sense. As argued in Thomas Kuhn's *The Structure of Scientific Revolutions*, 2nd edition (Chicago, IL: University of Chicago Press, 1970), scientific progress is typically made only when scientists "internalize" particular principles and techniques, uncritically using them to investigate nature. According to Kuhn's account, scientific change is less a matter of changing individuals' minds as it is a matter of older generations literally dying out and new generations – with new commitments – taking their places.

[24] See, for instance, Appiah's comment quoted in footnote 33 in Chapter 2. For a more neutral version of liberalism, see Jeff Spinner, *The Boundaries of Citizenship: Race, Ethnicity, and Nationality in the Liberal State* (Baltimore, MD: Johns Hopkins University Press, 1994).

[25] It is interesting to note that when Gutmann (in *Democratic Education*, p. 106) describes how a model of civic education would be implemented, she cites a case in which students engaged in a Socratic-style discussion of the morality of the United States' dropping atomic bombs on Japan. As reported, the students did engage in the kind of thoughtful debate that Gutmann encourages. But it is worth noting that the conclusions they reached – if they in fact reached any at all – were *not* reported. This is, of course, to be expected, but one should wonder what the result would be if the value of deliberation itself were the subject of discussion. (The case was cited from Diane Ravitch's *The Schools We Deserve: Reflections on the Educational Crises of Our Times*, New York: Basic Books, 1985, p. 288.)

to listen to what reason tells them. But it is also quite possible that they can't even *hear* what reason has to say. The ability to be moved by an argument – to be troubled by a fallacy, an inconsistency in one's beliefs, or an unjustified assertion – is an acquired disposition that itself demands training and support. If only a rational education can create these dispositions, how is this process supposed to get started?

5.2. IN PRAISE OF A "USEFUL PAST"

Operating within the constraints that Gutmann imposes sharply limits both the expected effectiveness and applicability of civic education. This, of course, is not just a problem for Gutmann's particular account, but of *any* proposal that focuses on deliberation and rationality. This assessment echoes that of William Galston, who claims that:

On the level of theory, liberalism takes sides in a series of disputes about the meaning of equality, freedom, and the human good – disputes that cannot be regarded as definitively settled from a philosophic point of view. On the practical level, *very few individuals will come to embrace the core commitments of liberal society through a process of rational inquiry.*[26]

The fact that rational means are unlikely to achieve our aims in civic education is not, however, reason to abandon hope, for Galston goes on to propose what he claims is a more effective method of delivering liberal values – rhetoric:

If children are to be brought to accept these [liberal] commitments as valid and binding, it can only be through a pedagogy that is far more rhetorical than rational. For example, rigorous historical research will almost certainly vindicate complex "revisionist" accounts of key figures in American history. Civic education, however, requires a more noble, moralizing history: a pantheon of heroes who confer legitimacy on central institutions and constitute worthy objects of emulation.[27]

The "moralizing history" envisioned by Galston can be seen as providing citizens with what Robert K. Fullinwider has called a "usable past," one that they can use as a body of moral and civil exemplars to guide

---

[26] Galston, "Civic Education in the Liberal State," p. 91; emphasis added.
[27] Ibid. Note that Galston's main objection to Gutmann is *not* at the level of implementation, but concerns what he considers her overly restrictive requirements.

their own lives.[28] It is a presentation of history explicitly formulated to help develop a particular kind of character and set of dispositions in citizens.

Many will recoil at the suggestion that we use history for political or social purposes, quite justly pointing out the possible abuses of this authority.[29] The obvious risk is that allowing "ulterior motives" – motives other than the desire to uncover the truth, no matter what it may be – to affect the content of the historical record threatens to open the door to all kinds of abuses. As Fullinwider has argued, however, the mere existence of an ulterior motive like this is not sufficient to reject "useful pasts." Indeed, this criticism is often motivated by the very same kind of ulterior motive, that is, the belief that the social objectives we *ought* to embrace are best pursued by a "disinterested' history."[30]

5.2.1. Useful Pasts, Liberal Purposes

Recognizing this point about ulterior motives opens the door to a non-pejorative view of useful pasts. But it is important that we not go too far in this direction, for if the blanket condemnation of politically expedient history is unwarranted, abuses are still quite possible. In order to put useful pasts to use for liberal purposes, we need some way to discriminate between those that are innocuous from those that are not.

In the present context, a candidate for a "useful past" is a political veil – a representation of history for an explicitly political purpose. Thus, the conditions of legitimate veils described in section 3.4 give us the theoretical framework to assess and criticize these veils in terms of content, translucency, and consent:

- *Content*: Is the representation of historical events counterproductive to liberal purposes? "Useful pasts" will often present historical

---

[28] Robert K. Fullinwider, "Patriotic History," in *Public Education in a Multicultural Society: Policy, Theory, Critique*, ed. Robert K. Fullinwider (Cambridge: Cambridge University Press, 1996), pp. 203–27.

[29] See, for instance, Diane Ravitch, "The Plight of History in American Schools," in *Historical Literacy: The Case for History in American Education*, ed. Paul Gagnon (New York: Macmillan, 1989) and Emily R. Gill, *Becoming Free: Autonomy and Diversity in the Liberal Polity* (Lawrence, KS: University of Kansas, 2001), p. 226.

[30] Fullinwider, "Patriotic History," p. 209. This seems clearly to be Gutmann's position, since the reason we encourage open and rational discourse is because such discourse tends to produce the kinds of rational and deliberative citizens we want in a democracy.

figures as heroic or as virtuous for particular reasons or traits. Such a history will clearly fail the "content" condition if a figure is portrayed as virtuous because she exemplifies illiberal characteristics.

- *Translucency*: Does the state actively discourage or prohibit interested parties from learning more about the actual history? If it does, then the veil is opaque.
- *(Hypothetical) Consent*: How far is the representation from the actual details of the historical event? This assessment can be made in terms of the expected reactions of individuals who are *first* given the useful version of history and *then* learn the truth. If they see the useful version as a false but plausible simplification of the truth, the condition for consent is satisfied.

The popular images of America's founding, for instance, provide a "useful past" for Americans. As commonly represented, the founders themselves form a vivid and compelling cast of characters, each of whom has a special talent or ability that perfectly complements those of the others.[31] The founding itself is reduced from a snarl of contingency to a coherent storyline rising from the Boston Tea Party to Paul Revere's ride and the "shot heard 'round the world," peaking at the Declaration of Independence, and then arcing gracefully, inevitably down again to Yorktown and victory, finally coming to rest with the ratification of the Constitution.

This is incomplete history, to be sure – some might say even fabricated or deceptive history. The central figures are but stylized versions of complex, even contradictory men; the storyline, only the crudest approximation to the actual events. But its simplicity is part of what makes it a *useful* history. The caricatures of Washington, Jefferson, and others give citizens *models* of different aspects of citizenship free of messy personal foibles that might obscure the special virtues that each character exemplifies.

The simplicity of the narrative serves a similar function. It leaves no room for anything to have happened but what *did* happen, lending a kind of inevitability to the country's origins. What the founders

---

[31] The composition of this cast is as old as classical mythology and legends of epic quests and as current as the stock characters of action/adventure films such as *The Guns of Navarone, The Magnificent Seven,* or *Saving Private Ryan*. Here, the wise sage (Franklin), the eloquent visionary (Jefferson), and the unpredictable hothead (Adams) challenge the great power (Great Britain) under the command of their prudent and resolute leader (Washington).

themselves knew to be a fortunate but highly improbable event becomes, when seen in this particular way, part of the natural course of history. Such a view is a "useful past" that instills a feeling of uniqueness and special purpose in Americans.[32]

From the point of view of a liberal, is there anything wrong with presenting this version of history? Given the criteria for assessing liberal veils that I have outlined, the main complication involves the assessment of (hypothetical) consent. That is, nothing in the *content* of this representation seems to conflict with liberalism's core values, so at least on that count it is unobjectionable. Neither does a consideration of transparency offer grounds for objecting to such a presentation of history, for in the United States, at least, there are numerous opportunities for learning details about the lives of these figures and the events of the Revolutionary period.

More complicated is the third condition, *consent*. The problem we face here is determining when we can say that those who act and form beliefs on the basis of a literally false and intentionally designed representation of the past have been manipulated. That the representation is known to fail to match to reality perfectly is no objection, of course – *no* history is liable to meet *that* standard.

The criterion given in section 3.4 allows us to draw finer distinctions among intentional misrepresentations, rather than lumping them all together as objectionable deceptions. Rather than just asking, "Does the veil misrepresent the object?" we consider a hypothetical situation: How would one who had first been given the veil react if she were subsequently given the truth. Is learning the truth disillusioning? If so, we have reason to think that the veil violates the consent requirement. If it is *not* disillusioning, however, the difference between representation and fact is innocuous.

Justifying such hypothetical judgments is, admittedly, no trivial matter.[33] But while there are highly problematic situations, there are plenty of other, relatively uncontroversial cases. For instance, someone whose

---

[32] At the same time, the air of inevitability about American democracy carries a certain risk of fostering complacency. As noted in Joseph J. Ellis, *Passionate Sage: The Character and Legacy of John Adams* (New York: W.W. Norton, 1993), this point was recognized by at least one of the founders, John Adams.

[33] See David Lewis's *Counterfactuals* (Cambridge, MA: Harvard University Press, 1973) and Robert Stalnaker's *Inquiry* (Cambridge, MA: MIT Press, 1987) for two perspectives on assessing counterfactual claims and some of the philosophical problems involved.

impression of the Ku Klux Klan is informed solely by, say, *The Birth of a Nation* will inevitably be disillusioned once she grasps the facts. A child of the Depression who grew up with a highly idealized vision of Franklin Roosevelt, on the other hand, has no reason to revise his opinion about FDR's greatness as a leader when the facts are finally recognized. Either way, the initial belief results from a misrepresentation, but the difference between the two is apparent. In the latter case, the facts vindicate the myth; we see in the truth what the myth correctly captures. In the former, the myth evaporates in light of the truth, like a fog burned off by the sun.

5.2.2. *Truth in False History*

The preceding examples suggest how we can explicate the intuitive distinction we draw between innocuous idealizations and abuses of history in terms of the (hypothetical) effect of seeing through the veil. The "useful" version of the founding of the United States provides a second illustration of this point. Consider, for instance, the portrait that Parson Weems presents in his *Life of Washington*:

Washington was pious as Numa, just as Aristides, temperate as Epictetus, patriotic as Regulus. In giving public trusts, impartial as Severus; in victory, modest as Scipio – prudent as Fabius, rapid as Marcellus, undaunted as Hannibal, as Cincinnatus disinterested, to liberty firm as Cato, and respectful of the laws as Socrates.[34]

This image reduces Washington from a flesh-and-blood man to quite literally a list of virtues – piety, temperance, modesty, law-abidingness. He is reduced to a secular republican symbol, with his character defined in reference to the fixed points of classical civic heroes.

Now compare this to a more realistic description of Washington. Among other things, he managed in 1754 to set off a worldwide conflict between the great powers of Europe, fell for the wife of a neighboring planter, worked behind the back of his friend and ally, Lafayette, to foil his efforts to bring Canada into the Revolutionary War, and knowingly

---

[34] Quoted from Mason Locke Weems's *Life of Washington*, 1st edition, in Garry Wills, *Cincinnatus: George Washington and the Enlightenment* (Garden City, NY: Doubleday & Company, 1984), p. 35.

conspired both to subvert the Articles of Confederation and to hide the minutes of the (illegal) Constitutional Convention from the public.[35]

The truth (or at least these *parts* of the truth) is hardly the stuff of Weems's legends. Remarkably, though, learning these facts seems hardly to make a dent in a fair assessment of Washington. Indeed, as impressive Washington appears in *fiction*, he emerges in truth as even *greater*. Garry Wills has observed that political myths often represent the founders of states as men immune to the intoxicating effects of power. Washington did the myth one better by actually walking away, first from the chance to be king, then after two terms as president:

Washington left of his own free will, living up to the legends only approximated by mythical figures. The man whose life began in an obscure scuffle of the major European powers fulfilled, at last, classical Europe's dream of a figure who might create a state without ensnaring himself in its very structure.[36]

In this case, it seems to me quite clear that the truth is *not* disillusioning, for when we peer behind the façade of the myth, we find the truth is essentially more of the same. I would add that the same appears to be true when we consider the images of other founders. In each case, the surface image is clearly false, but false in the way an insightful caricature is. Those who would dismiss these images as deceptions would do well to consider Wills's appraisal of Parson Weems's work:

Those who mock Weems as a pious biographer have mistaken his genre.... Weems gives us the meaning of Washington in a set of symbols, not following narrative logic at all. He was not recording events, but fashioning an icon. And Weems's book not only found more readers than the stilted epics from Connecticut [which also mythologized Washington] did; it had more, and more truthful, things to tell those readers.[37]

Wills's point here is simple, but profound: To fault an *icon* for failing to be *biography* is to commit a kind of category mistake. Only the most obtusely literal-minded would deny that Picasso's *Guernica* captures the true terror and helplessness of modern warfare simply because of the painting's Cubist style. In the same way, once we see that symbols and myths are a different kind of thing from biography, we can appreciate

---

[35] Garry Wills, *Certain Trumpets: The Call of Leaders* (New York: Simon & Schuster, 1994), pp. 148–52.
[36] Ibid., p. 153.
[37] Wills, *Cincinnatus*, p. 37.

that they, too, can express the truth, albeit in a way quite distinct from the way "factual" history does.

This insight into the difference between how symbols and factual history express the truth presents an even more interesting possibility: Symbols may, at times, be *superior* to explicit historical accounts in conveying the truth. Weems's profile of Washington, seeming at first to be no more than a crude reduction of a man, succeeds as few "truthful" biographies could to draw attention both to Washington and his virtues without compromising his true nature. The truth of the matter, we might say, is sometimes better conveyed by a fiction rather than by the whole, messy truth itself.

5.2.3. *Useful Pasts as Civic Ideals – The Myth of the Melting Pot*

The crucial consideration in the preceding discussion was the difference between what the veil indicates and the facts being veiled. In the case of the Washington myth, what mattered was how successfully that simplified myth captured the qualities of an actual person. In this section, I consider another case of a veil that, while misrepresenting the past in a literal sense, does so in a way that I believe is compatible with liberal principle.

One of the basic problems that all but the most authoritarian polities face is that of fostering a level of solidarity among its citizens. At a minimum, citizens must treat each other as entitled to whatever rights and protections the state affords to its citizens without being forced to do so. This sense of cohesion is, according to Mill, a key component of any notion of common citizenship:

We mean *a principle of sympathy*, not of hostility; of union, and not of separation. We mean a feeling of common interest among those who live under the same natural or historical boundaries. We mean, that one part of the community do not consider themselves as foreigners with regard to another part; that they set a value on their connexion; feel that they are one people, that their lot is cast together, that evil to any of their fellow-countrymen is evil to themselves; and do not desire selfishly to free themselves from their share of any common inconvenience by severing the connexion.[38]

[38] Mill, *Mill on Bentham and Coleridge*, p. 124. In the same spirit, Rawls insists "The Law of Peoples starts with the need for common sympathies, no matter what their source may be" (*The Law of Peoples*, Cambridge, MA: Harvard University Press, 1999, pp. 24–5).

5.2. In Praise of a "Useful Past"

A natural way to promote this kind of solidarity is to encourage citizens to regard themselves as sharing some important feature that binds them together. According to Mill, for instance:

[T]he condition of the permanent political society has been found to be, the existence, in some form or other, of the feeling of allegiance, or loyalty.... This feeling may attach itself to ... a common God or gods ... to certain persons ... or finally ... it may attach itself to the principles of individual freedom and political and social equality.[39]

In highly homogeneous societies, for instance, long standing cultural or ethnic similarities may be sufficient to provide this without any further effort. In highly diverse societies (such as the United States), the problem is much more acute, since there is simply more "competition" for ways of identifying oneself, for example, along ethnic, religious, or cultural differences.

Given the importance of finding a way to promote a common identity, a history that represents the United States as an amicable "melting pot" of different groups is particularly useful. The melting pot conjures the image of differences being broken down to form a unity; raw materials of all kinds poured into the pot flow out as a smooth, undifferentiated mass.

For an extreme example of this image, consider the following description of a bizarre "melting pot" ritual performed in 1916 at the Ford Motor Company English School:

The "Melting Pot" exercises were dramatic in the extreme: A deckhand came down the gang plank of the ocean liner, represented in canvas facsimile.

"What cargo?" was the hail he received. "About 230 hunkies," he called back. "Send 'em along and we'll see what the melting pot will do for them," said the other and from the ship came a line of immigrants, in the poor garments of their native lands. Into the gaping pot they went. Then six instructors of the Ford school, with long ladles, started stirring. "Stir! Stir!" urged the superintendent of the school. The six bent to greater efforts. From the pot fluttered a flag, held high, then the first of the finished product of the pot appeared, waving his hat. The crowd cheered as he mounted the edge and came down the steps on the side. Many others followed him, gathering in two groups on each side of the cauldron. In contrast to the shabby rags they wore when they were unloaded from the ship, all wore neat suits. They were American in looks. And ask anyone of them what nationality he is, and the reply will come quickly, "American!"

---

[39] Mill, *Mill on Bentham and Coleridge*, p. 122.

"Polish-American?" you might ask. "No, American," would be the answer. For they are taught in the Ford school that the hyphen is a minus sign.[40]

Today, of course, a ritual of this sort is almost unimaginable. Not only is it insulting to say that to be "good Americans," immigrants *must* surrender entirely their ethnic identities, it is wildly implausible to suggest as a descriptive claim that immigrants have ever in fact entirely shed their ethnic identities to become "unhyphenated Americans."[41]

Even in its less extreme forms, we have good reasons to think the melting pot is literally a *myth*: Instead of the blending of different cultures and traditions suggested by the melting pot metaphor, the U.S. population is increasingly a collection of distinct subpopulations, with more diversity *between* ethnic, linguistic, or cultural groups than *within* those same groups. If our interest is in the melting pot as a literal description of the United States, it leaves much to be desired. But as we have seen with respect to the mythology surrounding historical figures, this may be the wrong attitude to take when assessing such things. It may instead be that the myth's most important function – and its ultimate justification – was never as a literally true description at all.

The myths surrounding a historical figure, I have argued, serve to frame the civic virtues of a Washington or Lincoln and present them in an inspiring, unambiguous, yet truthful way. The melting pot myth serves essentially the same function: In a broad sense, each affects our *future* course by representing our *past* in a particular way. Myths about the founders help us to orient ourselves by defining our starting point or original purposes. The myth of the American melting pot, too, presents us with a story of *how things have always been* – immigrants to America have *always* taken on the special qualities or essence of Americans, with

---

[40] This description was originally printed in the Ford Motor Company paper, the *Ford Times*, and reprinted in Werner Sollors, *Beyond Ethnicity: Consent and Descent in American Culture* (Oxford, UK: Oxford University Press, 1990).
[41] For more on the myth of the melting pot, see the *Washington Post* series on trends in immigration and assimilation by William Booth ("One Nation, Indivisible: Is it History?; Soon, No Single Group Will Comprise Majority," February 22, 1998, p. A1; "The Myth of the Melting Pot: America's Racial and Ethnic Divide," July 13, 1998, p. A1); and by Michael Fletcher ("In Rapidly Changing L.A., a Sense of Future Conflicts," April 7, 1998, p. A1; "Patrolling the Crossroads of Schools, Discrimination; Education's Civil Rights Chief Stands in Political Hot Spot," December 28, 1998, p. A1). See also Steven E. Schier, "From Melting Pot to Centrifuge: Immigrants and American Politics," *Brookings Report*, Vol. 20, No. 1, Winter 2002 (Washington, DC: Brookings Institution).

the result that there is something that all Americans have in common and binds them together in common cause.

The need for something of this kind doesn't guarantee we are entitled to use *any* convenient means to acquire it. Here, just as when we considered the mythology surrounding civic heroes, we face a problem of assessing the legitimacy of a veil – in this case, a representation of that special property underlying civic unity. Once again, this calls for considering the three conditions of content, transparency, and consent. And, just as we found in the case of the Washington myth, the most difficult of these to assess is the consent clause.[42]

In the preceding discussion, we found that one way for the (hypothetical) consent condition to be satisfied is if the myth, although literally false, accurately represents the facts being veiled, with this being particularly clear in the case of Washington. Veils like the present one, however, stretch the limits of verisimilitude between veil and object almost to the breaking point: A caricature of FDR captures the spirit of the man in a truthful, albeit nonliteral way. It seems another thing entirely to think that a sketch of a *nonexisting* entity (Santa Claus or the Tooth Fairy) can be truthful in even that nonliteral sense.

Can myths like the melting pot *ever* qualify as legitimate for liberal states? In part, the justification of myths of this kind turns on there being a rationale for them; they support important civic values that the unadorned truth would not. That bluntly utilitarian argument by itself is *not*, however, sufficient to legitimize such a veil. The crucial additional factor concerns a judgment about the likely effects of first being given the veil and then seeing through it. Here we can frame the issue in the following way: The purpose of the myth is to foster solidarity among citizens. The relevant question to ask is whether seeing through the veil is likely to promote that end further, or is likely to be counterproductive, leading to further divisions. If myths that fail even to be figuratively accurate have a hope of legitimacy, then there must be myths of this sort that, once seen through, will not lead to this kind of disenchantment.

Some versions of the melting pot myth will clearly fail this condition. For instance, the "Melting Pot Ritual" described previously suggests

---

[42] With respect to content, there is nothing in the promotion of a sense of civic unity per se that is incompatible with liberal principles; thus, a myth like the melting pot satisfies that condition. Likewise, it satisfies the condition of transparency, since there are no enforced impediments to learning the facts about processes of assimilation.

a particularly implausible homogeneity: Americans *look* a certain way. What happens when an immigrant or a child who first comes to believe this myth finally learns that it is false? One likely reaction is to infer that there is no interesting feature in common among all Americans, nothing that binds them together. Alternatively, one might also conclude that those who fail to live up to this standard are not genuinely American. Either way, however, the most likely result of seeing through the veil is disenchantment – the unity and solidarity that the veil promises turns out to be an empty one.

Significantly, however, not all such veils suffer from this defect. The standard used by the Ford Motor Company in the early twentieth century is far too superficial to be anything but disenchanting. But rejecting such superficial criteria doesn't mean that we refuse to search for that special quality that puts the *unum* in *e pluribus unum*. On the contrary, the *need* for some kind of common civic identity suggests that we are likely to find in the future (as we do in the past) a series of candidates for the lowest common denominator for inclusion, each serving for a time to provide a past that suited the present's needs, and each revisable over time.

Although the self-identifying characteristic of Americans is likely to change in unpredictable ways over time as it responds to unpredictable events, we can anticipate at least some generalities to hold. For instance, the impossibility of finding any plausible superficial "essence" for Americans (such as the neat suits and "American looks" on the Polish immigrants in the previous example) means the candidates will almost invariably be highly abstract ones like a commitment to a set of formal principles, a cause, or something as vague as "the American Way."

These abstract conditions for self-identity can be seen as weakening the requisite conditions. Immigrants from Southeast Asia or Africa will *never* be able to join the "club" if membership is limited to Western European stock; devout Muslims and Buddhists are left out if Judeo-Christianity is the necessary condition. Weakening the conditions in this way widens the range of individuals who can be included. A purely formal condition (for example, having the appropriate naturalization papers filed) could be the weakest condition imaginable, since it depends on an easily manipulated property – documentation – rather than on a more robust one like lineage, appearance, belief, or culture. Such a criterion may appear particularly attractive if, as seems increasingly plausible, Americans share *no* distinctive feature.

The problem is that while such a criterion can be satisfied by a wide range of people, it is not one that is likely to have the emotive force sufficient to fire a people to action. Traits that are rare or that are determined by birth rather than choice – being a member of the Nso tribe, being a Roman Catholic, an Orthodox Jew, or a Lutheran from the Upper Midwest – can be very powerful motivators. It is harder to imagine traits that are pervasive or easily acquired – having a driver's license, a social security number, or birth certificate – having a similar effect.[43]

More generally, the motivating capacity of these criteria appears to be inversely proportional to their inclusiveness. Such criteria form, as it were, a series of concentric circles, with the innermost circle representing traits that have great emotive intensity but are also highly exclusive. The innermost concentric circle includes exclusive kinship relations, for example, "We are the Winnebago, from one father and mother," or, "We are DAR." As we move farther out, criteria become more inclusive, but they also lose motivational force. The outermost circle represents appeals to the universal, our common humanity. The emotive force is low but it appeals to many beyond cultural, religious, geographical, ethnic, and racial backgrounds and boundaries.

The challenge raised by diversity concerns the tension between inclusiveness and motivation. To err on the side of inclusiveness is to fail to engage the citizenry; we may be appealing to features genuinely shared by citizens, but these features are too ethereal to unite. To err in the opposite direction is to engage a portion of the population, but to leave behind the rest. What we want is to strike just the right balance between these two extremes, and it is in terms of this balance (rather than descriptive accuracy) that we should judge the various criteria proposed as "defining" the character of the citizenry.

When Americans characterize themselves as standing for fair play and equality, as uniquely optimistic, as "the last great hope of mankind," they are not just making a (self-serving) descriptive claim – which may

---

[43] Note that the significance of particular traits may often depend on the contrast between traits. In populations that are both isolated and predominantly Protestant, for instance, it may not be effective to appeal to citizens' being Protestant. If, however, that same population lived amidst other religious groups, such appeals would be much more likely to be effective. In the same way, the fact that I share the same official documents with millions of my fellow Cameroonians carries no special bond between us when we meet *there*; things are quite different when we meet on the streets of Boston.

or may not be true. More importantly, they are making a statement of purpose, and it is this purpose that connects them to other Americans who may have different ethnic roots, different religious beliefs, and dramatically different ways of life. It is quite plausible that as descriptive claims, *no* characterizations of what it is to be an American can stand scrutiny. But that will not stop Americans from looking elsewhere for some other candidate; particular versions of the melting pot will come and go, but as long as America has a discernable identity, some such myth will be around. And as I have argued previously, not only can liberals live with this reality, they can use it to promote their own purposes.

5.3. CIVIC EDUCATION BEYOND THE CLASSROOM

In designing a course of civic education, it is important that we strike the right balance between rational and emotional appeals. On one hand, citizens in a liberal state must be equipped with the deliberative skills and dispositions needed to pursue their aims in life intelligently and effectively. Thus, an essential part of preparing citizens is to develop their abilities to evaluate arguments and assess evidence. On the other hand, developing those skills and dispositions (along with the philosophically controversial values that are central to liberalism) in citizens requires that we see people as *more* than merely rational agents. Effective civic education, then, demands that we stand with one foot in the world of reason, the other in the more primitive one of feeling, emotion, and sentiment.

Even when we recognize the importance of striking this balance, however, it may be tempting to restrict concerns for civic education to formal lessons in civics, usually delivered in the form of courses similar to normal academic subjects like history or English. This reflects a tradition (at least in the United States) of placing the burden of civic education on educational institutions. For instance, the constitution of the Commonwealth of Massachusetts both identifies the primary goals of such education, and places the responsibility for achieving those goals with schools:

[I]t shall be the duty of legislatures and magistrates, in all future periods of this commonwealth, to cherish the interests of literature and the sciences, and all seminaries of them; ... to encourage private associations and public institutions; ... to countenance and inculcate the principles of humanity and general benevolence, public and private charity, sincerity, good humor, and all social affections, and generous sentiments among the people.[44]

In the same spirit, Justice Felix Frankfurter, in a Supreme Court decision *(Minersville School District v. Gobitis)*, defended the right of the state to require the performance of civic rituals in schools, arguing that:

The ultimate foundation of a free society is the building tie of cohesive sentiment. Such a sentiment is fostered by all those agencies of the mind and spirit which may serve to gather up the tradition of a people, transmit them from generation to generation, and thereby create that continuity of a treasured common life which constitutes a civilization. . . . The influences which help towards a common feeling for the common country are manifold. Some may seem harsh and others no doubt foolish. Surely, however, the end is legitimate.[45]

As both Justice Frankfurter and the authors of Massachusetts's Constitution recognized, schools are not *just* for academic training, but also have a role to play in instilling social and civic dispositions of various kinds – the willingness to hold their representatives and civic leaders accountable for their actions, to participate in policy recommendation and scrutiny, and to think of and treat their fellow citizens in particular ways.

This classroom-based approach is what I have referred to as *deliberative* civic education. In its narrowest sense, this component focuses on providing future citizens with facts about their history, constitutional order, and other governmental processes. More broadly, deliberative civic education aims to give students the intellectual skills needed to be a good citizen of a liberal state in the very way that Gutmann's own approach to civic education does.

In light of the limitations of this approach, I claim it needs to be complemented with what I call *demonstrative* civic education. This type of civic education provides citizens (and future citizens) with civic exemplars and inspiring representations of virtues, weaving these into everyday life rather than making them explicit. To use Gutmann's terminology, whereas deliberative civic education is a *conscious* social process, its demonstrative counterpart is an *unconscious* one. It is this complementary factor that provides the background for liberal democratic reason that enables citizens to elect and hold their representatives and civic

[44] *Constitution of the Commonwealth of Massachusetts*, Chapter V, Section II.
[45] Quoted in Robert Paul Wolff, *The Poverty of Liberalism* (Boston, MA, Beacon Press, 1968), pp. 72–3.

leaders accountable for their actions as well as to participate actively in policy decisions.

Each of these components has a role to play in the traditional civics classroom. On the deliberative side, children must be provided with information about the constitutional order as well as their civic rights and responsibilities. On the demonstrative side, these explicit lessons should be interwoven with inspiring (but legitimate) veils that unobtrusively form a civic narrative that gives a basic structure and content to the subject's judgments. A sound civic education curriculum would be a mix of these components that instills the foundations for rational deliberation by appeals to veils while at the same time nurturing the deliberative skills needed in the citizenry of a stable and thriving liberal polity.

All this is consistent with the traditional classroom-based approach to civic education. To limit their use to the classroom, however, would deprive us of some of the most effective means of supporting the qualities required of citizens of a thriving and stable liberal state. Recognizing the cumulative effect of veils on the character of citizens suggests that what goes on within the civics classroom is no more important than the images, representations, and exemplars that citizens of all ages find everyday in their own lives.[46] Issues related to civic education, then, crop up in many different contexts – not merely in the content of civics curricula and textbooks, but also in a wide range of decisions regarding the public expression of institutions, historical narratives, symbols, and traditions.

In theory, for instance, the public image of politicians might justly be considered irrelevant when we choose our leaders. Competency and knowledge, we like to believe, ought to trump anything as superficial as charm and personality (or the lack thereof). And yet we often find that competency and knowledge *alone* – while compelling under the cold light of reason – can be oddly impotent in real life. Why is this?

We look for many different qualities in leaders, including vision, ideals, and special expertise. But as Garry Wills has observed, great leaders have one extra thing in addition to all these – *followers*:

---

[46] One of the important figures in the planning and dedication of Gettysburg National Cemetery, Edward Everett, can be seen as advocating this kind of demonstrative civic education when he suggested that children be kept in instructive communion with the military cemetery by working on its upkeep (letter of November 28, 1863, Massachusetts Historical Society, in Garry Wills, *Lincoln at Gettysburg*, New York: Simon and Schuster, 1992, p. 70).

When [followers] are lacking, the best ideas, the strongest will, the most wonderful smile have no effect. When Shakespeare's Welsh seer, Owen Glendower, boasts that "I can call spirits from the vasty deep," Hotspur deflates him with the commonsense answer: "Why, so can I, or so can anyone. But will they come when you do call them?" *It is not the noblest call that gets answered, but the answerable call.*[47]

Wills argues that the gift of great elected leaders like FDR or Lincoln is *not* that they were the most intelligent or visionary politicians of their time. Rather, they had the ability to anticipate where the people were willing to go and use this understanding not (as a cynic might say) simply to rush to the front of the crowd, but to attract followers, those they could engage in a way that moved them *of their own volition* in the desired direction.[48]

Leading and following are, claims Wills, two parts of an interaction in which neither part is passive, and each emerges changed:

Coercion is not leadership, any more than is mesmerism. Followers cannot be automatons. The totalitarian jailer who drugs a prisoner into confession of a crime has not *led* him to some shared view of reality.[49]

A leader composes an image of herself that, in the prevailing circumstance, engenders a willingness to follow.[50] Usually this image involves a literal picture of some kind – a visual style that appeals quite directly to humans' natural ability to pick up on subtle cues and body language.[51] In genuinely effective leaders, it is unlikely that this image will be *just* a façade, yet if we are serious about putting political ideals to work in the real world, the "packaging" of those ideals is an essential consideration. Flouting basic moral standards, maintaining a disinterested academic

[47] Wills, *Certain Trumpets*, p. 13; emphasis added.
[48] This kind of leadership has what I have elsewhere referred to as *living legitimacy*. This understanding of legitimacy is defined in terms of the integration of political arrangements and everyday life, rather than in terms of high-level or abstract philosophical principles. For details, see Ajume H. Wingo, "Living Legitimacy: A New Approach to Good Government in Africa," *New England Journal of Public Policy*, Vol. 16, No. 2 (Spring/Summer 2001), pp. 49–71.
[49] Wills, *Certain Trumpets*, pp. 18–19.
[50] Ibid., p. 274.
[51] Describing FDR's uncanny control of his image in this sense, Wills writes:

His delivery was superb. He had studied people's reactions to his every move. He used theatrical props to rivet attention on this upper body. His pince-nez, his long cigarette holder, the cock of his head, his expansive gestures, his navy cape, his crumpled hats – all were calculated for effect (ibid., p. 30).

aloofness, appearing "disconnected" from the concerns of ordinary people, giving people a vague sense of being "uncomfortable in one's own skin" – all these are consistent with brilliance and vision. They are not, however, the qualities that make one's call an answerable one.

Wills' analysis of leadership dovetails nicely with my general framework of veil politics. Each stresses the need to make use of the resources at hand to achieve one's goals: Leaders lead by appealing to what their followers *already* value. Veil politics generalizes this insight. At the same time, the interactive relationship between leaders and followers described by Wills is a useful illustration of the participatory nature of liberal polities that I discussed in section 4.2. That is, consideration of these and other debates over symbols help to show how citizens can – in ways direct and indirect, conscious and unconscious – reshape and redefine political veils in ways that underwrite the legitimacy of such veils.

Political image is but one relatively superficial feature that takes on new importance and interest once we see the essential roles that these "merely symbolic" elements play. In the following section, I discuss two particular examples that illustrate how an appreciation of the role of veils in civic education may inform public debate.

5.3.1. Civic Monuments and Memorials

As a descriptive claim, it is obvious that "merely symbolic" issues often generate strong passions. Witness, for instance, the recent debates over public funding of controversial art or the debate over the representation of the *Enola Gay* display at the Smithsonian Museum.[52] My discussion of veils indicates that these debates are not necessarily quibbles over aesthetics or even over historical events, but are part of a process of creating and altering veils that in turn helps to shape civic purposes and the very character of citizens in a deep and profound way.

A fundamental theme of this book is, after all, that a society's values and aspirations are intimately bound up in its symbols. In that sense, arguments about who pays for what art or about the wording on a museum plaque are in fact deep and serious ones that go to the kind of

[52] Martin Harwit, *An Exhibit Denied: Lobbying the History of Enola Gay* (New York: Copernicus, 1996); Edward T. Linenthal and Tom Engelhardt (eds.), *History Wars: The Enola Gay and Other Battles for the American Past* (New York: Metropolitan, 1996).

people we claim (or hope) to be. Seen from that angle, it becomes clear why those who object most loudly to taxpayer support for controversial art are not allayed by reports of how small the amounts are; their objection is most commonly not a fiscal one at all, but one that is prompted by a view of what government is for and its proper bounds. In a similar way, the debate over the representation of the atomic bombing of Hiroshima is not in any interesting sense a historical one that can be resolved by a careful study of the conditions near the end of the war in the Pacific; it is over the "useful past" by which Americans represent themselves *to* themselves.

Monuments of the sort I have discussed previously can stir similar passions. As I described in section 3.4.1, for instance, there were strong, emotionally charged disagreements surrounding both the Vietnam Veterans and the FDR memorials. This is rather mysterious if they are simply works of public art, but quite explicable when we see them as political veils, designed and constructed with the explicitly political purpose of promoting a specific image of a person or event.

Occasions for commemorating heroes and events (either triumphs or tragedies) are thus opportunities for civic education. In constructing a memorial to a particular person or event, we have the chance to frame that person or event in a way that helps support some more general civic value. No society, of course, has ever needed a theory before doing this; in that sense, my account of veil politics doesn't promise us a new way of practicing politics. What it does provide is a new perspective on an age-old practice, a theoretical framework for analyzing veils that sheds light on how we can more effectively put this practice to work for liberal objectives.

In that respect, debates over the wisdom of placing new monuments on the Mall in Washington, D.C., are ones that involve issues of architectural integrity and aesthetics, but which also go well beyond those. Memorials to civic heroes act like signposts, telling the living in an uplifting manner where they have come from and where they are going.

The primary rationale for erecting a monument to an individual is usually to commemorate or honor his or her great achievements or historical significance. But the greatest of our monuments are more than tributes to an individual's deeds. Just as the greatness of Lincoln's Address at Gettysburg transcended the particular events of a specific battle, our finest memorials contribute most to civic education not by highlighting individual achievements and virtues, but by associating those achievements and virtues with the polity as a whole. The image of an admirable individual is put into service as an endorsement of the civic order in general.

Martin Luther King, Jr., for instance, has historical significance as an individual meriting fame, honor, and recognition. But as important a historical figure as King is, there are plenty of other figures who have also played important roles in the history of the United States who have not yet received the kind of public recognition accorded to King.

A cynic might regard this elevation of King to the civic pantheon either as the result of liberal white guilt or a kind of tokenism brought about by the pressure to recognize an African American. And to be fair, each of these factors probably *did* have a hand in outfitting a great civil rights leader with the trappings of an officially recognized civic icon. Yet, from the point of view of civic education, there are quite sound reasons for this kind of public recognition of King – and, arguably, good reasons to place a memorial in his honor on the Mall in Washington.

What sets King apart from many other great historical figures is that he has come to stand for civic values that transcend his own achievements. Figures like James Madison, Alexander Hamilton, and Ulysses S. Grant were, in their own ways, geniuses. But their genius lay in specific fields – in law, in government, in war – and what they have come to connote are at best *just* those special virtues. In contrast, King stands with a relative handful of others who have come to represent some of the most fundamental of American values.

Washington, Jefferson, and Lincoln each exemplify some of these values: the primacy of law, equality, the sacrifices demanded by the polity. King symbolizes a different, but equally important virtue: the possibility of civic redemption. Jefferson may *stand for* equality, but King shows us how to achieve it – not through bloodletting, but by peaceful, determined petitioning and civic protest. In bombing the Murrah Building in Oklahoma City, Timothy McVeigh chose to express his outrage at the (perceived) excesses of government with indiscriminate violence. King represents the alternative, in which genuine moral courage and faith in the fairness of the American people make progress and change possible.

Public figures like the Reverend King are an important source of material for veils. Important events can serve the same purpose. Consider, for example, the aftermath of the terrorist attacks of September 11, 2001, in New York, Pennsylvania, and the Pentagon. There, in the worst act of terrorism in U.S. history, we find the almost innate urge to memorialize. Fires were still burning beneath Ground Zero when the first talk of constructing memorials to the victims of the attack and the firefighters and police killed in attempting to rescue survivors began. Only six months after the attack, a month-long memorial of searchlights traced the outlines of the fallen Twin Towers.

What civic purpose could such a memorial serve? Memorials of this kind are most obviously a way of representing the dead – but they can do much, much more. We have already seen in section 4.3.2 how Lincoln seized the opportunity at Gettysburg, turning what might otherwise have been just a powerful symbol of a terrible struggle into one that reshaped the vision of the United States. Its emotional significance, brilliantly channeled by Lincoln for his own political vision, was what made irresistible his redefinition of the Union's origins and purpose.

The attacks of September 11 represent another opportunity. As I stressed in section 5.2, diverse liberal states have a particularly urgent need to instill a sense of unity and solidarity in their citizens.[53] A memorial dedicated to the attack's victims – those in the buildings and planes, and the firefighters, police officers, and ordinary people who put themselves in harm's way to help their fellow citizens – has the potential to teach and motivate citizens to act on the values of liberty and public virtues. In particular, these memorials can create participatory attitudes, motivating citizens to take position in defense of the ideals of their liberal democratic order.

Creating an artifact that is both effective and legitimate requires a blend of aesthetic judgment, historical perspective and timing, and above all, fluency in the existing symbols and traditions of the society. Earlier forms of the melting pot myth illustrate how exclusive veils run the risk of disenchanting large segments of the population, undermining both the legitimacy and the effectiveness of the veil. The recent controversy over the sculpture designed for the Brooklyn headquarters of the New York City Fire Department is a vivid illustration of the kind of sensitivity that is needed avoid such disenchantment.

Intended to honor the firefighters killed in the attack on the World Trade Center, the sculpture was based on a photograph taken by Thomas E. Franklin of three firefighters raising an American flag at Ground Zero. Such a memorial might seem quite promising as a motivational and unifying device. In perhaps as direct a way imaginable, it infuses a basic national symbol (the American flag) with the images of

---

[53] I again stress that such a unity needn't imply lockstep conformity; on the contrary, the solidarity appropriate for liberal states involves a mutual recognition among citizens to their right to determine their own lives.

firefighters (themselves new symbols of heroic service, courage, and sacrifice), all in the emotionally charged atmosphere of the terrorist attacks. It doesn't hurt that the statue and the photograph on which it is modeled is a historical echo of the famous Iwo Jima Memorial and the classic photograph on which *it* was modeled.

Examining the controversies that arose around this particular image highlights some of the pitfalls of veil design. The original photograph was of three *white* firefighters – not surprising, given that nearly 95 percent of New York City's firefighters were white. The sculpture, however, presented one as white, one as Hispanic, and one as black. Not surprisingly, emotions ran hot, with many firefighters, decrying how the statue misrepresented the original scene, charged the designers with *politicizing* history. Others, however, *praised* the statue as a tribute to diversity; in this spirit, a representative of black firefighters argued "the artistic expression of diversity would supersede any concern over factual correctness."[54]

In favor of the design we should acknowledge both the utility and the legitimacy of "useful pasts." Yet at the same time, it is hard to see the statue – which in all respects *other than* race perfectly matches the photograph – as anything but "doctored," altered for an obviously political purpose. Either of these "readings" of the sculpture is defensible, and that is precisely the problem with the sculpture as a veil. Veils symbolize other things; their purpose is to draw attention not to themselves, but to the ideals and values they represent. In that task, the statue is (at least for the present) a failure: The controversy in which it was cast has made it more of a divisive symbol than one of heroism, unity, *or* diversity.[55]

Acknowledging that the sculpture is a failed veil is not to reject the aim behind its design, but only to admit that its designers badly misjudged the situation. Much of the problem, I think, is due to the realistic nature of the image that on its face purports to represent the facts. A multivolume scholarly biography may "smooth the rough edges" of a historical figure in the same way that a political myth does. The difference between the two is that biography – like a highly realistic sculpture – invites a comparison to the facts in a way that obvious caricatures or abstractions

[54] Kevin James, quoted in Stephanie Gaskell's, "Flag-Raising Statue Stirs Debate over Authenticity," *Boston Globe*, January 12, 2002, p. A12.
[55] This is not to say that it will *forever* fail as a symbol of either unity or diversity (or both). Controversies have a way of fading in time, and it is easy to imagine that in the future the literal reading of the statue will have given way to the alternative.

do not. In this case, a more abstract image may have served the end more effectively than the highly realistic one actually used.

Abstraction, then, is a useful device for disabling a "debunking" instinct – the instinctive desire to check the truth of everything that looks like a factual claim. At the same time, this use of abstraction draws the onlooker in, demanding that she bring something of herself to the memorial, enhancing both the emotional impact and the inclusiveness of the veil. From that point of view, it is not surprising that Maya Lin's simple black wall of names is more moving than its conventional counterpart, nor that in the visitors to the Vietnam Veteran's Memorial you find people with radically different views of that war, all brought together by same object. The names on the wall are for some a roll call of warriors fallen in a noble struggle; for others, they are a list of victims of a tragic blunder. Despite these differences, each sees something in that one object that helps to heal the wounds left by a deeply divisive war.

5.3.2. Slavery Reparations

Decisions to erect monuments, decisions about whom and what we honor and the manner in which we do this, go well beyond merely aesthetic concerns. Looking at these objects through the lens of veil politics reveals the substantive nature of what may appear to be merely symbolic.

This connection between the substantive and the symbolic runs the other way as well. That is, what at first appears to be a disagreement about facts may be better conceived of as a dispute over symbols. Like the controversies over public funding of the arts and the *Enola Gay* display at the Smithsonian, many times we find disputes over symbols masquerading as arguments over fiscal priorities or historical facts.

Simply knowing what kind of dispute we face is, of course, no guarantee that we will find a resolution to it. But while it is no panacea, such information *is* important to know, for those concerning facts demand an approach very different from one appropriate to those disputes that are ultimately symbolic. Veil politics gives us a framework for taking arguments about symbols seriously. In doing so, it allows us to see what appear to be intractable and divisive factual disputes as differences over the significance of institutions, figures, and events. This new perspective gives us new opportunities for civic education. Seeing these differences as ultimately arising from veils is a way of bringing citizens into a discussion of the meaning of those veils and promoting their participation in the alteration of those veils.

One of these deeply divisive issues today is that of reparations for slavery. Taken literally, this is a demand for monetary compensation for past wrongs – wrongs done *by* people no longer alive *to* people long gone. The argument for reparations is essentially one from justice: If your great-grandmother stole my great-grandfather's watch and passed it down to you, would it be fair for you to keep what would have been mine had the original wrong not have been perpetrated? It seems implausible to say I have no claim on the watch, even though it never was actually mine. If this is right, a similar conclusion should also follow if, instead of a watch, we consider a far more important object – freedoms and opportunities stolen by slavery. True, one cannot return something like an opportunity or right in the way one can a watch, but one can compensate (via reparations) for their loss.

Of course, there are objections to such an argument. For instance, there seems to be an obvious difference between a stolen watch and stolen opportunities. A watch is something *owned* – its future ownership can be controlled through sale, trade, or inheritance. One has rights and opportunities, but if they can be said to be owned, they do not seem to be possessions in same way ordinary objects are.

The issue raised by this objection concerns a fact – specifically one concerning the status of the rights and opportunities denied to slaves. Other objections turn on other facts. How much are descendents of slaves owed? What would have happened had things been different? What moral fact justifies making unwitting beneficiaries of past injustices compensate others for wrongs done long before either party was born? Do whites descending from people who immigrated *after* the end of slavery have a smaller share to pay? Do blacks in the same situation deserve a smaller share of the reparations?

From a philosophical point of view, these are interesting questions, but I believe that framing the issue of reparations in terms of questions about facts like these may be deeply misleading. What they presume is that "the debt" for which reparations are owed is like the aforementioned stolen watch. If this is what the debt really is, who can imagine it ever being paid? But if *that* is not the debt, what could it be?

The real force behind the demand for reparations is not, I submit, a literal demand for cash payment. Rather, I claim that it is better understood as the demand for a place in the civic narrative: African Americans, among the very first settlers of America, feel left out of the national narratives of the land of their own birthright. Seen in this light, what initially seemed to be a legal issue can be seen as another opportunity for civic education.

To read current demands for reparations in this metaphorical sense may seem far-fetched. Yet it is striking how metaphorical a tone even the most outspoken advocates of reparations sound. For instance, in his book *The Debt*, Randall Robinson argues for a sweeping program of benefits to be paid to descendents of slaves. But while his argument maintains that these citizens are owed literal payment, his most poignant expression of the "debt" takes on a considerably more metaphorical tone when he reflects on the "official history" of the United States as depicted in the U.S. Capitol's Rotunda:

I looked straight up and immediately saw the callous irony, wondering if the slaves who had helped to erect the structure might have bristled at it as quickly as I. The monumental fresco covering 4,664 square feet had been painted by Constantino Brumidi in 1864, just as the hideous 246-year-old American institution of slavery was drawing to a close. According to the United States Capitol Historical Society, Brumidi's *Apotheosis of George Washington* had been painted in the eye of the Rotunda's dome to glorify "the character of George Washington and the principles upon which the United States was founded."

Today we think of these principles as including those of equality, diversity, and freedom. And yet when we look at this state sanctioned image, Robinson reports, we find an image at odds with those lofty ideals:

Symbolizing the carapace of American liberty, sixty-odd robed figures are arranged in heroic attitudes around the majestic Washington, before whom a white banner is unfurled bearing the Latin phrase *E Pluribus Unum*, or *one out of many*. But all of the *many* in the fresco are white.

Beyond these central figures, the only non-whites are Native Americans. Conspicuous by their absence are African Americans:

Although the practice of slavery lay heavily athwart the new country for most of the depicted age, the frieze presents nothing at all from this long, scarring period. *No Douglass. No Tubman. No slavery. No black, period. . . .* No reference is made to blacks or slavery in any of the paintings.[56]

---

[56] Randall Robinson, *The Debt: What America Owes to Blacks* (New York: Dutton, 2000, pp. 1–2); emphasis added.

To some, Robinson's point may seem ridiculously superficial; no one could seriously expect that a painting made in 1864 would present a picture of racial harmony. But this is *not* his point, and to read Robinson as insisting that the Rotunda be repainted or even that African Americans be *paid* for past slavery is to miss his more important point about the way blacks are excluded from the national narrative and the need to restructure that narrative to make room for them.

This feeling of exclusion is not something that can be simply "paid off" in any straightforward way. Paying *this* debt requires more than adding a few black faces to the Rotunda dome or even a massive "aid package" to African Americans. No, the debt to which Robinson alludes is one that can be "paid" only by impressing an entirely new appreciation of the role of African Americans on citizens white, black, and brown. This debt is one that will be paid only when the symbols and ceremonies of the land are seen by the citizenry and the world to include African Americans.[57]

Robinson and other advocates of reparations quite naturally speak in the language of dollars, damages, and litigation – perhaps because this is the only vocabulary Americans have for talking about justice and desert. That, however, misconstrues the nature of the issue. *Recognition* is the relevant issue, and while dollars and other forms of tangible material aid are important *parts* of recognition, they are only parts, and this is something we risk overlooking if we persist in thinking of the debt in literal dollar figures.[58]

The perspective on the "debt" that I am proposing is intended to counteract this risk by focusing our attention on the "symbolic debt" incurred by slavery. This should *not* be seen simply as a way to achieve justice on the cheap, for the deep changes in attitude for which it calls are bound to make serious demands. Financial support, special efforts to improve education, and programs designed to open new opportunities all have roles to play in this process. But in providing these, it is important that we recognize that the steps we take to make good America's promise of equality and freedom must, beyond providing material goods, provide a

---

[57] For an argument along these lines, see Glenn Loury's *The Anatomy of Racial Inequality* (Cambridge, MA: Harvard University Press, 2001), especially Chapter 4. See also his "Little to Gain, Much to Lose," in *Black Issues in Higher Education*, Vol. 18, No. 19, November 8, 2001, pp. 136.

[58] Lani Guiner, a Harvard Law professor, has presented arguments for proportionate representations that could be understood in this light as well.

narrative that includes all Americans and recognizes their contributions and value.

5.4. CIVIC EDUCATION BEYOND THE LIBERAL STATE

The problems of civic education are traditionally regarded as domestic ones, ones that arise within a state and center on instilling in its own citizens the values and habits needed to sustain the polity. My focus has, therefore, been on carving out a space within liberal states for the use of veils that harnesses the powerful forces of veils while at the same time respecting liberal principles.

Veil politics, I have argued, provides a useful theoretical framework for thinking about civic education while at the same time directing our attention toward factors that, as a purely practical matter, are effective in shaping the character of citizens. In addition, this framework helps us both to see opportunities for civic education in many of the problems that arise everyday and to recognize ways in which we can integrate civic lessons into those situations.

Liberal states have, however, concerns beyond merely these domestic ones. Among these are their relationships with other states and communities, either for the purpose of spreading and sustaining of liberalism abroad, or for the most basic aim of self-preservation. In this last section, I suggest how the framework of veil politics that I have presented in a domestic context informs judgments across national boundaries.

The most obvious forms of interstate relations are those of overt conflict – war – or of some kind of bargaining or trading relationship. Each of these is a method by which states engage one another. In interesting ways, each is an extension of how states might engage with their own citizens: The process of bargaining is analogous to appealing to an individual's rational judgment, while that of war is an application of brute force to get the desired response.

In the case of states dealing with their own citizens, we have seen that each of these approaches suffers from serious limitations. The process of bargaining is too much subject to the caprice of reason, while that of war is both inherently unstable and incompatible with liberal principles. Indeed, if anything, the factors that generate the main problems for civic education within a state – the fact of diversity, the existence of deep disagreements over values and principles, and the need to forge a community despite these differences – become even more acute when we consider relations between states. The world grows smaller every day, thrusting people of very different social, religious, and economic backgrounds into contact with ever-greater frequency. Groups once separated by oceans, mountains, and deserts are now linked by CNN, airliners, and cell phones.

In a provocative 1993 essay, Samuel Huntington argued that for the foreseeable future, the main conflicts in the world will be between civilizations, large groups of people bound together by religious, ethnic, and cultural backgrounds, rather than nation-states, which are defined in terms of common political principles.[59] Nation-states, of course, will continue to be the major political actors (as they have been for two hundred years), but the causes of conflicts will be the result of different civilizations with different values and worldviews coming into contact. With rapid travel and easy access to almost instantaneous communication, contact of this sort is bound to become more common.[60]

Such contact holds the promise of greater understanding and appreciation of others. But the attacks of September 11, 2001, also indicate the frightening possibilities of this smaller world. The United States has long enjoyed an enviable geographical position: a friendly neighbor in Canada to her north, a weak one in Mexico to her south, and two great moats to the east and west. As those tragic events clearly demonstrated, those days are over. Terrorism in the Middle East, diamond-induced wars in Sierra Leone, human rights violations in China, drug production in Columbia – all these spill over to affect liberal democracies. And through computers, television, and the Internet, the poor increasingly see themselves as unequal to a handful of rich states of the West. The result (justified or not) is resentment, with the very technology and symbols of the wealth and power of the West turned against it.

In light of this, liberal democracies cannot afford to be indifferent to the rest of the world. But at the same time, the methods that Western states typically use in dealing with other states seem ill-suited to the

---

[59] Samuel P. Huntington, "A Clash of Civilizations?" *Foreign Affairs*, Vol. 72, No. 3 (Summer 1993), pp. 22–49.

[60] I hasten to point out that one doesn't have to embrace the particular lines that Huntington claims demarcates civilizations to appreciate his insight into the importance of groups broader than nation-states. Huntington is quite aware that his "civilization-based paradigm" is an abstraction, and as such, bound to oversimplify how the world really is. But as I have argued in section 5.2, such literally false abstractions may capture the truth far better than any 1:1 scale map does.

challenge they face. Blunt tools have their uses; against certain kinds of localized threats, military force can be effective; in others, economic incentives are a powerful motivation when decision makers are concerned about economic interests. But military power is no panacea; smart bombs and cruise missiles are ideal for destroying a factory or barracks, but considerably less effective against a belief or credo. More frightening perhaps is the fact that the new style of terrorist exemplified in Osama Bin Laden – educated, well-off individuals who consciously reject what the Western liberal states have to offer – literally deny the kind of reason that the West takes for granted.

"Faith and family, blood and belief," Huntington claims, "are what people identify with and what they will fight and die for."[61] These are the factors that underlie many of the deep differences in aims and values we find in the world today. Unfortunately, they are also differences that rational discourse is unlikely to dislodge, that cannot be forced out at gunpoint, that will not be bought off by a higher standard of living. We operate in a world in which we *have* to deal with people who "play," as it were, on dramatically different fields of aims and values.

Veil politics gives us the conceptual tools needed in these circumstances, for the same primitive forces that cannot be beaten out, reasoned away, or bought are the very factors that veil politics would have us use in political practice. Just as veil politics gives the state the means effectively and legitimately to affect the character and disposition of citizens, so too does it give states on two sides of such a divide a bridge, a way to interact with other states when neither force nor open appeals to reason are likely to succeed.

Huntington offered a rather bleak vision of the near future, one in which incommensurable cultures ("the West and the Rest") engage in constant skirmishing at their points of contact – especially between the West and Islamic and Confucian states.[62] In the short term, he counsels that the West take a wary attitude toward the Rest, consolidating its power, maintaining military superiority over Asia and the Middle East, and strengthening ties to potential allies like Russia.

No one can expect that the differences between, say, an atheist professor of comparative literature in the United States and a radical Muslim cleric in Saudi Arabia will disappear overnight. Insofar as the differences

---

[61] Samuel P. Huntington, "If Not Civilizations, What?" *Foreign Affairs*, Vol. 72, No. 5 (November/December 1993), p. 194.
[62] Huntington, "A Clash of Civilizations?" p. 48.

between the West and the East reflect those differences, Huntington's pessimism about the short term seems quite justified. But there is also, I believe, hope. As Huntington observes, our problem is not to erase the differences between cultures and civilizations, but to find a way for them to coexist. The atheist professor may differ in her view of the world just as dramatically from her conservative Southern Baptist neighbor as she does from the radical cleric. What brings the former pair together is a set of shared veils – symbols that give them a plot of common ground – and it is the possibility of finding some such common plot for other differing parties that is the promise of veil politics.

Bibliography

Abramsom, Daniel 1996. "Maya Lin and the 1960s: Monuments, Time Lines and Minimalism," *Critical Inquiry*, Vol. 22, No. 4, 1996, pp. 679–709.

Anderson, Benedict 1990. *Imagined Communities: Reflections on the Origin and Spread of Nationalism* (London: Verso, 1990).

Appiah, Kwame Anthony 1992. *In My Father's House* (New York: Oxford University Press, 1992).

_____ 1996. "Culture, Subculture, Multiculturalism," in *Public Education in a Multicultural Society*, ed. Robert K. Fullinwider (New York: Cambridge University Press, 1996), pp. 65–89.

Bailyn, Bernard 1967. *Ideological Origins of the American Revolution* (Cambridge, MA: Harvard University Press, 1967).

Bass, S. Jonathan 2001. *Blessed Are the Peacemakers: Martin Luther King, Jr., Eight White Religious Leaders, and the "Letter from Birmingham Jail"* (Baton Rouge, LA: LSU Press, 2001).

Becker, Carl L. 1922. *The Declaration of Independence: A Study in the History of Political Ideas* (New York: Vintage, 1922).

Berlin, Isaiah 1969. "Two Concepts of Liberty," in *Four Essays on Liberty* (Oxford, UK: Oxford University Press, 1969), pp. 118–72.

Booth, William 1998a. "One Nation, Indivisible: Is it History?; Soon, No Single Group Will Comprise Majority," *Washington Post*, February 22, 1998, p. A1.

_____ 1998b. "The Myth of the Melting Pot: America's Racial and Ethnic Divide," *Washington Post*, July 13, 1998, p. A1.

Burke, Edmund 1955. *Reflections on the Revolution in France*, ed. Thomas H. D. Mahoney (Indianapolis, IN: Bobbs-Merrill, 1955).

Callan, Eamonn 1992. "Tradition and Integrity in Moral Education," *American Journal of Education* 101 (November 1992), pp. 94, 96.

_____ 1994. "Beyond Sentimental Education," *American Journal of Education* 102 (1994), pp. 190–221.

_____ 1996. "Political Liberalism and Political Education," *Review of Politics* 58 (Winter 1996), pp. 5–33.

Carroll, Lewis 1994. *Through the Looking Glass* (New York: Puffin Books, 1994).

Cassirer, Ernst 1979. *Symbol, Myth, and Culture: Essays and Lectures of Ernst Cassirer 1935–1945*, ed. Donald P. Verene (New Haven, CT: Yale University Press, 1979).

Davidson, Philip 1941. *Propaganda and the American Revolution, 1763–1783* (Chapel Hill, NC: University of North Carolina Press, 1941).

Dees, Morris 1988. "Law Center to Build Civil Rights Memorial," *Law Report of the Southern Poverty Law Center*, October 4, 1988, pp. 1, 3.

Dewey, Donald O. 1970. *Marshall v. Jefferson: The Political Background of Marbury v. Madison* (New York: Knopf, 1970).

Diamond, Jared 1997. *Guns, Germs and Steel: The Fates of Human Societies* (New York: W. W. Norton, 1997).

Donald, David Herbert 1961. "Getting Right with Lincoln," in *Lincoln Reconsidered: Essays on the Civil War Era*, 3rd edition (New York: Vintage Books, 1961), pp. 3–14.

Douglass, Frederick "The Meaning of July Fourth for a Negro," in Philip S. Foner, ed., *The Life and Writings of Frederick Douglass*, Vol. 2; *Pre–Civil War Decades, 1850–1860* (New York: International Publishers Co., 1950), pp. 181–204.

Downe, R. S. and Elizabeth Telfer 1971. "Autonomy," *Philosophy* 46 (1971), pp. 293–301.

Ellis, Joseph 1993. *Passionate Sage: The Character and Legacy of John Adams* (New York: W. W. Norton, 1993).

_____ 1996. *American Sphinx: The Character of Thomas Jefferson* (New York: Vintage Books, 1996).

Fletcher, George P. 2001. *Our Secret Constitution: How Lincoln Redefined American Democracy* (New York: Oxford University Press, 2001).

Fletcher, Michael 1998a. "In Rapidly Changing L.A., a Sense of Future Conflicts," *Washington Post*, April 7, 1998, p. A1.

_____ 1998b. "Patrolling the Crossroads of Schools, Discrimination; Education's Civil Rights Chief Stands in Political Hot Spot," *Washington Post*, December 28, 1998, p. A1.

Frankel, Charles 1953. "Liberalism and Political Symbols," *Antioch Review* 13 (Summer 1953), pp. 351–60.

Fukuyama, Francis 1992. *The End of History and the Last Man* (New York: Avon Books, 1992).

Fullinwider, Robert K. 1996. "Patriotic History," in *Public Education in a Multicultural Society*, ed. Robert K. Fullinwider (New York: Cambridge University Press, 1996), pp. 203–27.

Gadamer, Hans-Georg 1994. *Truth and Methods* (New York: Continuum, 1994).

Galston, William 1989. "Civic Education in the Liberal State," in *Liberalism and the Moral Life*, ed. Nancy L. Rosenblum (Cambridge, MA: Harvard University Press, 1989), pp. 89–101.

_____ 1991. *Liberal Purposes* (New York: Cambridge University Press, 1991).

_____ 1995. "Two Concepts of Liberalism," *Ethics* 105 (April 1995), pp. 516–34.

_____ 1996. "Value Pluralism and Political Liberalism," *Report from the Institute for Philosophy and Public Policy*, Vol. 16, No. 2 (Spring 1996), pp. 7–13.

Garhart, Tom 1982. "A Better Way to Honor Viet Vets," *Washington Post*, November 15, 1982, pp. B1, B6.

Gaskell, Stephanie 2002. "Flag-Raising Statue Stirs Debate over Authenticity," *Boston Globe*, January 12, 2002, p. A12.

Gill, Emily R. 2001. *Becoming Free: Autonomy and Diversity in the Liberal Polity* (Lawrence, KS: University of Kansas, 2001).

Guest, Stephan and Alan Milne (eds.) 1985. *Equality and Discrimination: Essays in Freedom and Justice* (Philadelphia, PA: Coronet Books, 1985).

Gutmann, Amy 1987. *Democratic Education* (Princeton, NJ: Princeton University Press, 1987).

_____ 1989. "Undemocratic Education," in *Liberalism and the Moral Life*, ed. Nancy L. Rosenblum (Cambridge, MA: Harvard University Press, 1989), pp. 71–88.

_____ 1995. "Civic Education and Social Diversity," *Ethics* 105 (April 1995), pp. 557–79.

Gyekye, Kwame 1978. *An Essay on African Philosophical Thought* (Philadelphia, PA: Temple University Press, 1978).

Hampshire, Stuart 1993. "Liberalism: The New Twist," *New York Review of Books* 40 (August 12, 1993), pp. 44–6.

Hampton, Jean 1994. "The Common Faith of Liberalism," *Pacific Philosophical Quarterly* 75 (1994), pp. 186–216.

Harwit, Martin 1996. *An Exhibit Denied: Lobbying the History of Enola Gay* (New York: Copernicus, 1996).

Haskins, George L. and Herbert A. Johnson 1981. *Foundations of Power: John Marshall, 1801–1815* (New York: Macmillan, 1981).

Herman, Edward and Noam Chomsky 2002. *Manufacturing Consent: The Political Economy of the Mass Media* (New York: Pantheon Books, 2002).

Hobbes, Thomas 1962. *Leviathan: Or the Matter, Forme and Power of a Commonwealth Ecclesiasticall and Civil*, ed. Michael Oakshott (New York: Macmillan, 1962).

Hume, David 1978. *A Treatise of Human Nature*, ed. L. A. Selby-Bigge (Oxford, UK: Clarendon Press, 1978).

Huntington, Samuel P. 1991. *The Third Wave: Democratization in the Late Twentieth Century* (Norman, OK: University of Oklahoma Press, 1991).

_____ 1993a. "The Clash of Civilizations?" *Foreign Affairs*, Vol. 72, No. 3 (Summer 1993), pp. 22–49.

_____ 1993b. "If Not Civilization, What?" *Foreign Affairs*, Vol. 72, No. 5 (November/December 1993), pp. 186–94.

Kant, Immanuel 1958. *Groundwork of the Metaphysics of Morals*, trans. H. J. Paton (New York: Harper & Row, 1958).

Kendall, Willmoore 1971. *Willmoore Kendall Contra Mundum*, ed. Nellie D. Kendall (New Rochelle, NY: Arlington House, 1971).

Kendall, Willmoore and George W. Carey 1970. *The Basic Symbols of the American Political Tradition* (Baton Rouge, LA: LSU Press, 1970).

Kertzer, David I. 1988. *Ritual, Politics and Power* (New Haven, CT: Yale University Press, 1988).

Kuhn, Thomas 1970. *The Structure of Scientific Revolutions*, 2nd edition (Chicago, IL: University of Chicago Press, 1970).

Levinson, Meira 1999. *The Demands of Liberal Education* (Oxford, UK: Clarendon, 1999).

Levinson, Sanford 1998. *Written in Stone* (Durham, NC: Duke University Press, 1998).

Lewis, David 1969. *Convention: A Philosophical Study* (Cambridge, MA: Harvard University Press, 1969).

———— 1973. *Counterfactuals* (Cambridge, MA: Harvard University Press, 1973).

Linenthal, Edward T. and Tom Engelhardt (eds.) 1996. *History Wars: The Enola Gay and Other Battles for the American Past* (New York: Metropolitan, 1996).

Loury, Glenn 2002. *The Anatomy of Racial Inequality* (Cambridge, MA: Harvard University Press, 2002).

———— 2001. "Little to Gain, Much to Lose," in *Black Issues in Higher Education*, Vol. 18, No. 19, November 8, 2001, p. 36.

MacIntyre, Alistair 1981. *After Virtue* (Notre Dame, IN: Notre Dame Press, 1981).

Maimonides, Moses 1963. *The Guide for the Perplexed*, Vol. 1, trans. Shlomo Pines (Chicago, IL: University of Chicago Press, 1963).

Mansbridge, Jane 1980. *Beyond Adversarial Democracy* (Chicago, IL: University of Chicago Press, 1980).

Mill, John Stuart 1950. *Mill on Bentham and Coleridge* (Westport, CT: Greenwood Press, 1950).

———— 1993. *Utilitarianism, On Liberty, Considerations on Representative Government, Remarks on Bentham's Philosophy*, ed. Geraint Williams (London: J. M. Dent, 1993).

Miller, John C. 1960. *Sam Adams, Pioneer in Propaganda* (Stanford, CA: Stanford University Press, 1960).

Mitgang, Herbert (ed.) 1994. *Abraham Lincoln: A Press Portrait* (Athens, GA: University of Georgia Press, 1994).

Nagel, Thomas 1986. *The View from Nowhere* (Oxford, UK: Oxford University Press, 1986).

Nozick, Robert 1974. *Anarchy, State, and Utopia* (New York: Basic Books, 1974).

Oakshott, Michael 1962. *Rationalism in Politics* (Indianapolis, IN: Liberty Press, 1962).

Okin, Susan Moller 1989. *Justice, Gender, and the Family* (New York: Basic Books, 1989).

Orwell, George 1944. "As I Please," *Tribune*, July 7, 1944, p. 257. Quoted in Michael Shelden, *Orwell* (New York: HarperCollins, 1990), p. 367.

Pascal, Blaise 1966. *Pensées*, trans. A. J. Krailsheimer (London: Penguin, 1966).

Peters, R. S. 1972. "Freedom and Development of the Free Man," in *Education and the Development of Reason*, ed. R. F. Dearden (London: Routlege and Kegan Paul, 1972).

Ravitch, Diane 1985. *The Schools We Deserve: Reflections on the Educational Crises of Our Times* (New York: Basic Books, 1985).

———— 1989. "The Plight of History in American Schools," in *Historical Literacy: The Case for History in American Education*, ed. Paul Gagnon (New York: Macmillan, 1989).

Rawls, John 1971. *A Theory of Justice* (Cambridge, MA: Harvard University Press, 1971).

_____ 1980. "Kantian Constructivism in Moral Theory," *Journal of Philosophy* 77 (Summer 1980), pp. 515–72.

_____ 1987. "The Idea of an Overlapping Consensus," *Oxford Journal of Legal Studies* 7 (1987), pp. 1–25.

_____ 1993. *Political Liberalism* (New York: Columbia University Press, 1993).

_____ 1999. *The Law of Peoples* (Cambridge, MA: Harvard University Press, 1999).

Richburg, Kenneth B. 1997. *Out of America: A Black Man Confronts Africa* (New York: HarperCollins, 1997).

Robinson, Randall 2000. *The Debt: What America Owes to Blacks* (New York: Dutton, 2000).

Rousseau, Jean-Jacques 1982. *The Basic Political Writings*, trans. Donald A. Cress (Indianapolis, IN: Hackett, 1982).

Rude, George 1967. *Robespierre* (Englewood Cliffs, NJ: Prentice Hall, 1967).

Sandel, Michael J. 1996. *Liberalism and the Limits of Justice* (Cambridge, UK: Cambridge University Press, 1996).

Scanlon, Thomas 1972. "A Theory of Freedom of Expression," *Philosophy and Public Affairs* 1 (Winter 1972), pp. 204–26.

Scheffler, Samuel 1982. *The Rejection of Consequentialism* (Oxford, UK: Clarendon Press, 1982).

Schier, Steven E. 2002. "From Melting Pot to Centrifuge: Immigrants and American Politics," *Brookings Report*, Vol. 20, No. 1, Winter 2002 (Washington, DC: Brookings Institution).

Schmitt, Carl, 1986. *The Crisis of Parliamentary Democracy*, trans. Ellen Kennedy (Cambridge, MA: MIT Press, 1986).

Schumpeter, Joseph 1947. *Capitalism, Socialism, and Democracy*, 2nd edition (New York: Harper, 1947).

Sollors, Werner 1990. *Beyond Ethnicity: Consent and Descent in American Culture* (Oxford, UK: Oxford University Press, 1990).

Spinner, Jeff 1994. *The Boundaries of Citizenship: Race, Ethnicity, and Nationality in the Liberal State* (Baltimore, MD: Johns Hopkins University Press, 1994).

Stalnaker, Robert 1987. *Inquiry* (Cambridge, MA: MIT Press, 1987).

Stevenson, C. L. 1938. "Persuasive Definitions," *Mind*, Vol. 47, No. 187 (July 1938), pp. 331–50.

Strauss, Leo 1971. *Natural Right and History* (Chicago, IL: University of Chicago Press, 1971).

Strauss, Leo and Joseph Cropsey (eds.) 1987. *History of Political Philosophy*, 3rd edition (Chicago, IL: University of Chicago Press, 1987).

Tamir, Yael 1993. *Liberal Nationalism* (Princeton, NJ: Princeton University Press, 1993).

van Fraassen, Bas C. 1980. *The Scientific Image* (Oxford, UK: Clarenden Press, 1980).

Waldron, Jeremy 1985. "Indirect Discrimination," in *Equality and Discrimination: Essays in Freedom and Justice*, eds. Stephan Guest and Alan Milne (Philadelphia, PA: Coronet Books, 1985), pp. 93–100.

_____ 1987. "Theoretical Foundations of Liberalism," *Philosophical Quarterly*, Vol. 37, No. 147 (April 1987), pp. 127–50. Reprinted in *Liberal Rights: Collected Papers 1981–1991* (New York: Cambridge University Press, 1993), pp. 35–62.

_____ 1992. "Minority Culture and Cosmopolitan Alternative," *University of Michigan Journal of Law Reform* 25 (September 1992), pp. 751–93.

_____ 1996. "Multiculturalism and Melange," in *Public Education in a Multicultural Society*, ed. Robert K. Fullinwider (New York: Cambridge University Press, 1996), pp. 90–118.

Walzer, Michael 1967. "On the Role of Symbolism in Political Thought," *Political Science Quarterly*, Vol. 82, No. 2, (1967), pp. 191–204.

_____ 1987. *Interpretation and Social Criticism* (Cambridge, MA: Harvard University Press, 1987).

_____ 1988. *The Company of Critics* (New York: Basic Books, 1988).

Weberman, David 1996. "Heidegger and the Disclosive Character of Emotions," *Southern Journal of Philosophy* 3 (1996), pp. 379–410.

Wener, Leif 1995. "Political Liberalism: An Internal Critique," *Ethics* Vol. 106, No. 1 (October 1995), pp. 32–62.

Wilkerson, Isabel 1982. "'Art War' Erupts over Vietnam Veteran Memorial," *Washington Post*, July 8, 1982, p. D3.

Wills, Garry 1984. *Cincinnatus: George Washington and the Enlightenment* (Garden City, NY: Doubleday & Company, 1984).

_____ 1992. *Lincoln at Gettysburg: The Words That Remade America* (New York: Simon and Schuster, 1992).

_____ 1994. *Certain Trumpets: The Call of Leaders* (New York: Simon & Schuster, 1994).

Wingo, Ajume H. 1998. "African Art and the Aesthetics of Hiding and Revealing," *British Journal of Aesthetics*, Vol. 38, No. 3 (1998), pp. 251–64.

_____ 2001a. "Good Government is Accountability," in *Explorations in African Political Thought*, ed. Teodros Kiros (New York: Routledge and Kegan Paul, 2001).

_____ 2001b. "Living Legitimacy: A New Approach to Good Government in Africa," *New England Journal of Public Policy*, Vol. 16, No. 2 (Spring/Summer 2001), pp. 49–71.

Wiredu, Kwasi 1996. *Cultural Universals and Particulars* (Bloomington, IN: Indiana University Press, 1996).

Wolff, Robert Paul 1968. *The Poverty of Liberalism* (Boston, MA: Beacon Press, 1968).

_____ 1970. *In Defense of Anarchism* (New York: Harper & Row, 1970).

Zakaria, Fareed 1997. "The Rise of Illiberal Democracy," *Foreign Affairs*, Vol. 76, No. 6 (November/December 1997), pp. 22–43.

Index

abstraction, 139, 144n
Adams, John, 93
adornment, aesthetic, 6–7
aesthetics
    of hiding and revealing, 8
    of veiled object, 6
African Americans
    and Declaration of Independence,
        99–103
    invisibility in U.S. history, 141–2
ambiguity, of veils, 15
American Revolution, 92–4.
        see also Declaration of
        Independence
Americans
    self-characterization by, 129–30
    self-identification of, 128
anti-Semitism, 78–9
Appiah, K. Anthony, 45
Aquinas, Thomas, 20n
arcana imperii, 78
Aristotle, xiv, 11
artifacts. see also memorials
artistic expression vs.
        factual correctness
        of, 138
    creating, 137
    power of, 1–2
    socializing function of, 2
Aryan race, as myth, 78

autonomous agents, 50–2, 55
autonomy, 49–52
    concept of, 49–50
    and culture, 55–8, 88
    defined, 49
    education for, 111–13
    of individual, nonparticipatory
        regime as threat to, 88
    and nonrepression, 109–10,
        109n
    peace and, 53–4
    and rationality, 110
    through tradition, 56–8
    tradition and, 54–5
    veils as threat to, 15–16, 50, 52–4,
        103–4

Bailyn, Bernard, 92–4
The Basic Symbols of the American
        Political Tradition (Kendall
        and Carey), 98
Becker, Carl L., 93
behavior, symbolic factors affecting,
        49
Bill of Rights, 89
Bin Laden, Osama, 145
Bolingbroke, Henry St. John, 92
bombing, in Oklahoma City, 136
Boucher, Jonathan, 93
Burgh, James, 92